The Design Index 5

FOR THE CORPORATE MANAGER

Credits / Copyright

Dust jacket illustration
Illustration de la jaquette
Schutzumschlagillustration

M Design

Divider page design
Design des pages de titre
Design der Länder-Seiten

Priscilla Teoh, FIE-JJA, Singapore

Production manager
Chef de production
Produktionsleiter

Bernard Vouillamoz, Geneva

Publisher
Editeur
Verlag

ROTOVISION SA
Route Suisse 9
CH–1295 Mies
Switzerland
Tel. (0)22-755 30 55
Tlx: 419 246 rovi ch
Fax: (0)22-755 40 72

Copyright

© 1991 ROTOVISION SA
ISBN 2-88046-123-5
Printed in Hong Kong

Content / Contenu / Inhalt

Portfolio Page Sales Agents

AMERICA
SCOTT & DAUGHTERS
940 North Highland Avenue
Los Angeles, California 90038
Tel. 800-547 2688
Fax: 213-856 4368
Contact: Suzanne Semnacher

ARGENTINA
DOCUMENTA SRL.
Aquiles Ferrario
Cordoba 612 entrepiso
1054 Buenos Aires
Tel. 1-322 9581
Fax: 1-111 879
Tlx: 24051 schnk ar

AUSTRALIA
ARMADILLO PUBLISHERS PTY LTD
205/207 Scotchmer Street
Fitzroy North
Victoria 3068
Tel. 03-489 95 59
Fax: 03-489 5576
Tlx: 30834 displa aa

AUSTRIA
Gudrun Tempelmann-Boehr
Am Rosenbaum 7
4006 Erkrath
Deutschland
Tel. 0211-25 32 46
          39 68 39
Fax: 0211-25 46 32

BELGIUM
SEDIP
Mr. P. de Vanssay / Mrs E. Wibaut
Rue Vanderkindere 318
1180 Bruxelles
Tel. 2-343 44 99
Fax: 2-343 79 51

BRAZIL
CASA ONO COMÉRCIO
E IMPORTAÇÃO LTDA.
Rua Fernão Dias 492 – Pinheiros
São Paulo
CEP 05427
Tel. 11-813 6522
Fax: 11-813 6921
Tlx: 11-80901 ono br

CANADA
CREATIVE SOURCE
WILCORD PUBLICATIONS LTD
511 King St. W, Suite 110
Toronto, Ontario
M5V 2Z4
Tel. (416) 599-5797
Fax: (416) 591-1630
Contact: Geoff Cannon

CHILI
BLACKBOX
M.H. Theurillat
Perez Valenzuela 1503
Santiago
Tel. 2-223 2869
Fax: 2-274 7520
Tlx: 645 330 booth

COLOMBIA
FONDO CULTURAL IBEROAMERICANO
H. Tinjaca
Calle 66 A N.º 16-41
Apartado 51340
Bogotá D.E.
Tel. 249 77 69
Fax: 283 02 65
          611 08 07

DENMARK
DANSK CELEBRATION
Danish Forlags Service
Orbækvej 739
52220 Odense SO
Tel. 65 97 24 06
Fax: 66 17 74 42
Contact: Helen Ramsdal

FINLAND
Leena Anttila
Kilonkallio 7 A
P.O. Box 50
02610 Espoo
Tel. 509 30 11
Fax: 59 20 49

FRANCE
STRATÉGIES
15 bis, rue Ernest-Renan
92130 Issy-les-Moulineaux
Tel. 1-40 93 01 02
Fax: 1-40 93 00 18
Contact: Catherine Lhéricel

GERMANY
SIEGMUND VERLAG
Christian Siegmund
Buxtehuder Strasse 31B
2151 Moisburg
Tel. 04165-60 01 04
Fax: 04165-68 83

HOLLAND
SEDIP
Mr. P. de Vanssay / Mrs E. Wibaut
Rue Vanderkindere 318
1180 Bruxelles
Belgium
Tel. 2-343 44 99
Fax: 2-343 79 51

HONG KONG
KENG SENG TRADING & CO.
David Chen
Loong San Building – Room 103
140-142 Connaught Road
Central
Hong Kong
Tel. 5-45 50 08
Fax: 5-41 40 25
Tlx: 64820 kshk hx

INDIA
GS BOOKS INTERNATIONAL
K.S. Ganesh
503 Amit Industrial Estate
61 Dr. S.S. Rao Road, Lalbaug
Bombay 400 012
Tel. 413 81 42
Tlx: 117 2336 baas in

INDONESIA
PT GRAFINDO INTER PRIMA
32 Kwitang Road
P.O. Box 4215
Jakarta
Tel. 21- 36 39 21
Fax: 21-858 18 06
Tlx: 45366 gps ia

ITALY
ROTOVISION SA
Route Suisse 9
CH–1295 Mies
Switzerland
Tel. (0)22-755 30 55
Fax: (0)22-755 40 72
Tlx: 419 246 rovi ch

JAPAN
ORION BOOKS
ORION SERVICE & TRADING
CO. LTD.
Hideo Kaneko
Papyrus Building
58 Kanda-Jimbocho 1-chome
Chiyoda-ku
Tokyo 101
Tel. 295 4008
Fax: 295 4366
Tlx: 24408 orionagy j

KOREA
DESIGN HOUSE
186-210 Jang-Choong-Dong
2-Ga, Choong-ku
100-392 Seoul
Tel. 275 6151
Fax: 275 7884

LUXEMBOURG
SEDIP
Mr. P. de Vanssay / Mrs E. Wibaut
Rue Vanderkindere 318
1180 Bruxelles
Belgium
Tel. 2-343 44 99
Fax: 2-343 79 51

MALAYSIA
FLO ENTERPRISE SDN. BHD.
Ong Kah Khin
42-A Jalan SS 21/58
Damansara Utama
Selangor
Tel. 03-718 7770
          718 7790
Fax: 03-718 6426

MEXICO
PRODUCCIÓN MGA S.A.
Marcela Gaxiola
Montes Cárpatos 210
Col. Lomas Virreyes
11000 México, D.F.
Tel. 540 20 76
Fax: 525 01 91

NEW ZEALAND
PROPAGANDA
123 Ponsonby Road
Ponsonby
Auckland
Tel. 09-781 582
Fax: 09-781 582
Contact: Stuart Shepherd

NORWAY
TW MARKETING
Thor Willy Bjerke
Fougstadsgate 22 B
0173 Oslo 1
Tel. 02-37 50 80
Fax: 02-37 73 20

PORTUGAL
LIBROS TÉCNICOS LDA.
Pedro Campos
Rua Herois Dadra 2-1.º DT
Damaia
2700 Amadora – Lisboa
Tel. 011-97 05 59
          97 24 39
Fax: 011-67 84 89

SINGAPORE
PAGE ONE – THE DESIGNER'S
BOOKSHOP PTE LTD
Mark Tan
6 Raffles Boulevard
03-128 Marina Square
Singapore 1030
Tel. 339 0288
Fax: 339 9828

SPAIN
ROVIRA ASOCIADOS SL
Calle Galileo 288 Entresuelo B
08024 Barcelona
Tel. 93-490 57 34
Fax: 93-490 16 62

SWEDEN
ROTOVISION SA
Route Suisse 9
CH–1295 Mies
Switzerland
Tel. (0)22-755 30 55
Fax: (0)22-755 40 72
Tlx: 419 246 rovi ch

SWITZERLAND
ROTOVISION SA
Route Suisse 9
CH–1295 Mies
Tel. (0)22-755 30 55
Fax: (0)22-755 40 72
Tlx: 419 246 rovi ch

THAILAND
AB PUBLICATIONS
Ramesh Shrestha
131/26-28 Sukhumvit 9
Bangkok 10110
Tel. 253 2561
Fax: 253 2561

TURKEY
ROTOVISION SA
Route Suisse 9
CH–1295 Mies
Tel. (0)22-755 30 55
Fax: (0)22-755 40 72
Tlx: 419 246 rovi ch

UNITED KINGDOM
ROTOVISION SA
c/o HOT SALES INTERNATIONAL LTD
35 Britannia Row
London N1 8QH
Tel. 071-226 1739
Fax: 071-226 1540

VENEZUELA
CONTEMPORÁNEA DE EDICIONES SRL
Luis Fernando Ramirez
Av. La Salle cruce con Lima
Edificic Irbia
Urb. Los Caobos
Apartado Aéreo
1020 Caracas
Tel. 2-782 2991
     2-782 3320
Fax: 2-782 3431
Tlx: 29105 armun

Index By Discipline

Display design

Environmental design

Graphic design

Industrial design

Interior design

Packaging design

Textile design

Product design

Geographical Alpha Index

Belgium
Belgique
Belgien

DECOBO 71
EDDY CORBEEL
Hovenierstraat 39
2800 Mechelen
Tel. +32-15-42 15 50
Fax: +32-15-42 29 06

DELTADESIGN ASSOCIATES 72
Consultant:
Bruno Anquinel
Nadine Tasquin
Madeliefjesstraat 48
1850 Grimbergen
Tel. 02-269 59 83
Fax: 02-269 76 24

HERMANN ADVERTISING 70
Kolonel Begaultlaan 15/3
3012 Leuven – Brussels
Tel. 32-16-22 24 91
Fax: 32-16-29 24 96

Agent in UK:
Michael Rynne (Device) London
Unit 8
A. Davis Industrial Estate
Somerlayton Road
London SW9 8ND
Tel. 44-7'-737 3983

Agent in Germany:
Eveline Varga
Sinkenweg 7
D-6057 Dietzenbach 1 – Frankfurt
Tel. 49-6074-31807

PINEAPPLE DESIGN S.A. 68-69
Rue de la Consolation 56 Troostraat
Bruxelles 1030 Brussels
Tel. 02-242 78 20
Fax: 02-242 96 40

LUC STRUYF & PARTNERS 67
Vijverstraat 1
1930 Zaventem
Tel. 02-720 62 96
Fax: 02-725 22 67

Brazil
Brésil
Brasilien

ART COMPANY DESIGN PROMOCIONAL LTDA. 190
Rua Bastos Pereira 454
CEP 04507 São Paulo SP
Tel. 011-887 00 20
        885 44 80
Fax: 011-884 01 40

DAP DESIGN 191
Rua Baluarte, 305
CEP 04549 São Paulo SP
Tel. 011-531 30 39

GAD-ARCHITECTURE AND DESIGN GROUP 192
Rua Eudoro Berlink 369
90420 Porto Alegre
Tel. 0512-30 28 74

Rua Visc. de Pirajá, 318/404
22410 Rio de Janeiro RJ
Tel. 021-521 50 95

Canada
Canada
Kanada

CRANWELL PIETRASIAK 202
9 Hazelton Avenue, 3rd Floor
Toronto, Ontario
Tel. (416) 975-1699
Fax: (416) 975-4031

GDC 203
400 Eastern Avenue
Toronto, Ontario
M4M 1B9
Tel. (416) 463-5782

JARS DESIGN 204-205
10 Ontario Ouest #903
Montréal, Québec
H2X 1Y6
Tél. (514) 844-0530

LEGOUPIL COMMUNICATIONS 206-207
424 rue Guy #200
Montréal, Québec
H3J 1S7
Tél. (514) 939-3379
Fax: (514) 939-3628

LE MOT DESSINÉ INC. 216
5890 Avenue Monkland #401
Montréal, Québec
H4A 1G2
Tél. (514) 485-1800
Fax: (514) 485-3034

REACTOR ART & DESIGN LTD 208-209
51 Camden Street
Toronto, Ontario
M5V 1V2
Tel. (416) 362-1913
Fax: (416) 362-6356

THE RIORDON DESIGN GROUP INC. 210-211
5945 Airport Road, Suite 195
Toronto, Ontario
L4V 1R9
Tel. (416) 271-0399
Fax: (416) 271-0256

R.K. STUDIOS 212-213
309 Wellesley Street East
Toronto, Ontario
M4X 1H2
Tel. (416) 964-6991

WOLF SCHELL DESIGN 214-215
1220 MacKay
Montréal, Québec
H3G 2H4
Tél. (514) 935-7098
Fax: (514) 935-8794

Chile
Chili
Chile

EDICIONES HERNAN GARFIAS LTDA. 194
Almirante Pastene 232
Providencia
Santiago
Tel. 46 55 95
        223 57 38
Fax: 56-2-46 55 95

WALKER DISEÑO 195
Regina Humeres 230
Santiago
Tel. 37 22 55
        37 97 19
Fax: 052-37 22 55

France
France
Frankreich

ARCHITRAL 110-111
28, rue Broca
75005 Paris
Tél. (1) 45 35 04 04
Fax: (1) 43 366 38 98
Télex: 205 616

CARRÉ NOIR 98-99
EUROPE:
Carré Noir S.A.
82-84, boulevard des Batignolles
75850 Paris Cedex 17
France
Tél. (1) 42 94 02 27
Fax: (1) 42 94 06 78
Télex: 281 237 F

NORTH AMERICA:
Carré Noir Inc New York
Morris Zand
244 Fifth Avenue
New York, NY 10001
USA
Tel. 212-645 0191
Fax: 212-645 1086

ASIA:
Agence Carré Noir Tokyo
Akasaka Q Building, 5/F
7-9-5 Akasaka
Minato-ku
Tokyo 107
Japan
Tel. 03-582 1201
Fax: 03-582 1202

CRABTREE HALL 102
70 Crabtree Lane
London SW6 6LT
Tel. 071-381 8755
Fax: 071-385 9575

DESGRIPPES & ASSOCIATES 91
18 bis, avenue de la Motte Picquet
75007 Paris
Tél. (1) 45 50 34 45
Fax: (1) 45 51 96 60

DESIGN STRATEGY S.A. 106-107
Villa Souchet
105, avenue Gambetta
75020 Paris
Tél. (1) 43 66 55 33
Fax: (1) 43 66 79 00
Télex: 213 620

DISTINCTIVE DESIGN ARDAIN 97
17, rue du Pont-aux-Choux
75003 Paris
Tél. (1) 48 04 77 70
Fax: (1) 48 04 39 26

ESPACE INTUITION 105
5, rue des Hospitalières Saint-Gervais
75004 Paris
Tél. (1) 42 71 08 12
Fax: (1) 42 71 13 72

LACOMBE, PINGAUD 94-95
7, rue Robert-Fleury
75015 Paris
Tél. (1) 45 67 01 04
Fax: (1) 45 67 81 37

LE CLAN DESIGN 92-93
61, rue Servan
75011 Paris
Tél. (1) 48 05 82 82
Fax: (1) 48 05 82 09

OVA'O 96
24, rue Feydeau
75002 Paris
Tél. (1) 40 28 00 92
Fax: (1) 40 28 00 93

PRÉFÉRENCE 100-101
16, rue Vézelay
75008 Paris
Tél. (1) 42 89 11 48
Fax: (1) 45 61 92 79

PGJ 104
1, rue d'Argenson
75008 Paris
Tél. (1) 42 68 08 45
Fax: (1) 42 68 01 21

PLAN CREATIF 102
10, rue Mercœur
75011 Paris
Tél. (1) 43 70 60 60
Fax: (1) 43 70 96 29

STYLE MARQUE 103
10, rue des Moulins
75001 Paris
Tél. (1) 42 96 16 78

VITRAC DESIGN 109
PARIS–MADRID–TOKYO
60, rue d'Avron
75020 Paris
Tél. (1) 40 24 08 00
Fax: (1) 40 24 08 12

Germany
Allemagne
Deutschland

GAUMER, OLAF 118-123
Holzhausenstrasse 22
6000 Frankfurt am Main 1
Neue Anschrift ab 1.1.1991:
Schumannstrasse 10
Tel. 069- 55 04 15
55 04 16
55 04 17
59 08 68
Fax: 069-596 23 53

SOKOLL UND KLANK DESIGN 114-115
Pöseldorfer Weg 7
2000 Hamburg 13
Tel. 040-410 17 13

WINDERLICH, WINDI 116-117
Eimsbütteler Chaussée 23
2000 Hamburg 20
Tel. 040- 43 17 08-0
Fax: 040-430 05 86

Holland
Hollande
Holland

BOZELL DESIGN 84-85
Bovenkerkerweg 2
1185 XE Amstelveen
Tel. 020-47 69 76
Fax: 020-47 71 91

CLAESSENS PRODUCT CONSULTANTS B.V. 76-77
Van Hengellaan 10
1217 AS Hilversum
Tel. 035-21 05 51
Fax: 035-21 71 62
Telex: 43071

HARRY & ELISABETH ELBERS DESIGN 83
Vaartweg 36
4731 RA Oudenbosch
Tel. 01652-16319
Fax: 01652-15204

KOPERDRAAD DESIGN / REKLAME 88
Noordereinde 13
P.O. Box 145
1243 ZJ 's Graveland
Tel. 035-6 34 35
Fax: 035-6 32 58

ANN MAES INDUSTRIAL DESIGN 86-87
Terlostraat 3
5571 KW Bergeyk
Tel. 04975-4455
Fax: 04975-4555

SAMENWERKENDE ONTWERPERS (SO DESIGN) 75
Herengracht 160
1016 BN Amsterdam
Tel. 020-624 05 47
Fax: 020-623 53 09

STEMPELS & OSTER 82
De Klencke 4
1083 HH Amsterdam-Buitenveldert
Tel. 020- 46 42 46
Fax: 020-661 29 21

MILLFORD–VAN DEN BERG DESIGN 80-81
Groot Haesebroekseweg 1
P.O. Box 56
2240 AB Wassenaar
Tel. 01751-1 91 00
Fax: 01751-1 36 85

VAN VELSEN 78-79
Laapersveld 41
1213 VB Hilversum
Tel. 035-23 27 05

Hong Kong
Hongkong
Hong Kong

TOMMY LI DESIGN & ASSOCIATES 19
221A Wanchai Road, 5th Floor
Hong Kong
Tel. 834 6312
        834 7332
Fax: 834 7032

INDEX TO ADVERTISER
REGENT PUBLISHING SERVICES 20
Hong Kong Office:
Call George Tai
REGENT PUBLISHING SERVICES LTD.
24th Floor, Federal Centre
77 Sheung On Street
Chai Wan
Hong Kong
Tel. 852-897 78 03
Fax: 852-558 72 09

New York Office:
Call Albert Yokum
REGENT PUBLISHING SERVICES LTD.
127 East 59th Street
New York, NY 10022, USA
Tel. 212-371 4506
Fax: 212-371 4609

London Office:
Call Gordon Beckwith
REGENT PUBLISHING SERVICES LTD.
4th Floor, 4 Brandon Road
London N7 9TP, UK
Tel. 071-607 3322
Fax: 071-700 4985

Indonesia
Indonésie
Indonesien

DWI SAPTA PRATAMA ADVERTISING 46-47
Office:
Kelapa Gading Boulevard TN 2/23
Kelapa Gading Permai
Jakarta 14240
Tel.   451 16 75
          471 08 14
Starko: 380 27 01
          36 11 01
          @1 03 27
Studio:
Jl. Ekor Kuning III/27
Rawamangun
Jakarta 13220
Tel.   489 46 65
          471 22 07
Fax: 489 02 92

GUA GRAPHIC 48-49
PT. GAJAH UTAMA AGUNG
Jl. Salembaraya I/20
Jakarta 10430
Tel.   021-33 11 60
Fax: 021-33 39 93
P.O. Box 83/KBYTB
Jakarta 12001

GUGUS GRAFIS 52
Jl. Pejompongan Raya No. 23
P.O. Box 35/JKPPJ
Jakarta 10210
Tel.   58 13 73
          58 35 62
Fax: 58 13 73

UMAR, ARMYN F. 51
AU GRAPHIC DESIGN
Jl. Ciasem IV/24
Kebayoran Baru
Jakarta Selatan
Tel.   021-71 70 38
Fax: 021-77 02 84

WINARSO – PROSPECT GRAPHIC HOUSE 50
Jl. Bumi Kemanggisan IV
Blok D1
Jakarta 11480
Tel. 549 35 09

Italy
Italie
Italien

ARDUINI & SALVEMINI 131
Via Ciro Menotti, 33
20129 Milano
Tel. 02-22 26 51
          294 099 94

BRAGGION, PAOLO 130
Via Giuseppe Verdi, 20
35010 Limena (Padova)
Tel. 049-76 73 57

Agents:
LUCATELLO S.p.A.
Via G. d'Annunzio, 75
31030 Biancade (Treviso)
Tel.   0422-8491 01
Fax: 0422-84 99 99
Telex: 410 595

MOBILEGNO FATTORI S.r.l.
Industria Mobili Componibili
Via Postumia Est
31042 Fagarè (Treviso)
Tel.   0422-79 00 16
          79 02 84
Fax: 0422-79 04 72

Korea
Corée
Korea

AHN GRAPHICS LTD. 34-35
1-34 Tongsung-dong
Chongno-gu
Seoul 110-510
Tel.   02-743 8065/6
          743 4154
          763 2320
Fax: 02-744 3251
Modem: 745 7209
Electronic Mail: ahn01dh
CompuServe: 72401, 1230

ALL COMMUNICATIONS 28-29
Red House 3, 4 Fl, 721 Banpo-dong
Seocho-gu
Seoul
Tel.   02-549 6440
          549 6441
Fax: 02-549 6441

CDR 37-40
666-5, Yoksam-dong
Kangnam-ku
Seoul
Tel.   02-557 3353
          557 3354
Fax: 02-557 5880

CROSSPOINT COMMUNICATION 24-25
564 Shinsa-Dong
Kangnam-ku
Seoul
Tel.   02-512 2283
          512 2284
          512 2285
Fax: 02-512 2286

DESIGN BRIDGE 26-27
32 F. Korea World Trade Center
159-1 Samsungdong Kangnamku
Seoul 135-729
Tel.   02-551 3271
Fax: 02-551 3275

HEXA INTERNATIONAL 30
208-18, Buam-dong
Jongro-gu
Seoul 110-021
Tel.   02-733 0445
Fax: 02-737 7704
Modem: 02-733 0446

INFINITE GROUP 41-44
12 F, Anguk Building
175-87, Anguk-Dong
Chongro-gu
Seoul
Tel.   736 7533–5
Fax: 737 6907

Korea
Corée
Korea

KIM, JAE-HYUN 31
Agent:
CROSS CULTURAL CENTER FOR ASIA
Hosan Building, 2F
709-8, Banpo-Dong
Seocho-ku
Seoul 137'040
Tel. 02-512 3948
512 3949
Fax: 02-512 3948

**SEOUL DESIGN CENTER
32-33**
Moon Hwa Building, 4F
47-15, 2 Ka, Jeo-Dong
Choong-ku
Seoul
Tel. 02-272 8646
272 8647
Fax: 02-278 8771

**SEOUL GRAPHIC CENTER
22-23**
The 5th, Seoul Graphic Center Bldg.
436-11, Chang-jeon Dong
Ma-po ku
Seoul 121-00
Tel. 324 5402
336 3074
Fax: 332-6706

Malaysia
Malaisie
Malaysia

**DYNAMIC IMAGE INC.
SDN. BHD. 57**
18-2 Medan Setia 2
Plaza Damansara
Bukit Damansara
50490 Kuala Lumpur
Tel. 03-256 1675
256 1678
256 1679
Fax: 03-256 1681

**FIXGO ADVERTISING (M)
SDN. BHD. 54-55**
28, 2nd Floor, Jalan SS 19/1D
Subang Jaya
47500 Petaling Jaya
Selangor
Tel. 03-733 6596
Fax: 03-733 1857

**FLO ENTERPRISE SDN. BHD.
58**
42-A Jalan SS 21/58
Damansara Utama
47400 Petaling Jaya
Selangor
Tel. 03-718 7770/90
Fax: 03-718 6426

TEH CHIN SENG, TONY 56
SENDIRIAN BERHAD
No. 21A SS 21/37
Damansara Utama
47400 Petaling Jaya
Selangor
Tel. 03-719 3000
03-717 2875
Fax: 603-717 2875

Portugal
Portugal
Portugal

AFINAL 139
R. Cándido de Figueiredo, 78, 2.º- Dt.º
1500 Lisboa
Tel. 78 82 81
74 19 46
Fax: 78 40 36

CARVALHO, DAVID DE 144
Trav. Conde da Ribeira 21-1.º Esq.
1300 Lisboa
Tel. 362 08 63

**JORGE CARVALHO &
LEONOR PERRY, LDA. 134**
Rua Morais Soares, 7-1.º Dto.
1900 Lisboa
Tel. 351-1-82 05 44
83 38 87
Fax: 351-1-82 55 81

COSTA, FILIPE 141
Seat: Av. do Uruguai, 34-7.º C
1500 Lisboa
Tel. 714 38 26

Atelier:
Complexo do Paço
Paço do Lumiar
1600 Lisboa
Tel. 758 73 51
Fax: 759 83 42
Telex: 60297

NOGUEIRA, HENRIQUE 137
Rua Alfredo Cunha, 217-1.º
Salas 5/6
4450 Matosinhos
Tel. 93 47 25
Fax: 93 86 40
Telex: 25211

**QUATRO PONTO QUATRO
142-143**
Rua José Magro
Lote 4 Traseiras
1300 Lisboa
Tel. 64 82 30
64 82 39
Fax: 64 90 80
Telex: 61606 QUAQUA P

SERISE EXPRESSO 135
Praceta Pintor José Félix
Lote 83 Loja Esq.
Reboleiro Sul
2700 Amadora
Tel. 0351-1-97 51 95
Fax: 0351-1-87 32 09
97 51 95

Spain
Espagne
Spanien

AR•17 162-163
MIGUEL ANGEL ANADON
Beethoven, 15-7.º, 4.ª
08021 Barcelona
Tel. 93-201 40 88
201 02 27
Fax: 93-209 37 43
Télex: 977 154 NERE-E

BCyM 160-161
Pau Claris, 97-1.º, 2.ª
08009 Barcelona
Tel. 93-318 14 28/78
Fax: 93-302 06 47

**ESTUDIO BERENGUER
146-147**
Aribau, 324 Entlo. C
08006 Barcelona
Tel. 93-200 49 85
Fax: 93-200 49 85

CAMALEON 164-165
Zurita, 18
50001 Zaragoza
Tel. 976-21 54 05
Fax: 976-23 01 59

**CUSIDO & COMELLA
168-169**
Còrsega 286, 2.º-2.ª
08008 Barcelona
Tel. 93-218 29 12
218 25 25
Fax: 93-237 98 21

**ANTONIO DIAZ &
ASOCIADOS, S.A. 154-155**
Avda. Dr. Federico Rubio y Galí, 67
28400 Madrid
Tel. 91-459 31 69
459 34 02
Fax: 91-450 93 32

**ESTUDIO DIGITAL GRÁFICO
S.A. 170-171**
Abtao, 25
28007 Madrid
Tel. 91-551 71 03/04
Fax: 91-433 27 66

**GARCÍA VEGA, JOSÉ MARÍA
174-175**
Irún, 9-4.º C
28008 Madrid
Tel. 91-248 79 08

**ARCADI MORADELL &
ASOCIADOS 152-153**
Paseo Bonanova 14, Torre A
08022 Barcelona
Tel. 93-211 51 44
211 53 04
Fax: 93-417 89 60

Singapore
Singapour
Singapur

Switzerland
Suisse
Schweiz

Thailand
Thaïlande
Thailand

INDEX TO ADVERTISER

United Kingdom
Grande-Bretagne
Grossbritannien

CREESE LEARMAN & KING 184-185
71-73 St. John Street
London EC1M 4AR
Tel. 071-253 2300
Fax: 071-251 8856

LACKIE NEWTON LTD 183
13/15 Circus Lane
Edinburgh EH3 6SU
Tel. 031-220 4141
Fax: 031-220 4004

THE YELLOW PENCIL COMPANY 187
2 Cosser Street
London SE1 7BU
Tel. 071-928 7801
Fax: 071-928 1419

United States
Etas-Unis
Vereinigte Staaten

BLACKDOG 220
MARK FOX
85 Liberty Ship Way #112
Sausalito, California 94965
Tel. 415-331 3294
Fax: 417-331 3296

BUTLER-HOME 218-219
940 North Highland Ave. Suite C
Los Angeles, California 90038
Tel. 213-469 8128

CHASE, MARGO 221
2255 Bancroft Avenue
Los Angeles, California 90039
Tel. 213-668 1055
Fax: 213-668 2470

CLARK/RUNKEL, INC. 222
KENNETH CLARK
2702 McKinney Avenue #203
Dallas, Texas 75204
Tel. 214-671 0999

DICKENS, HOLLY 224-225
612 North Michigan Avenue #710
Chicago, Illinois 60611
Tel. 312-280 0777
Fax: 312-280 1725

DIGITAL ART 223
TIM ALT
3000 South Robertson Blvd. #260
Los Angeles, California 90034
Tel. 213-836 7631
Fax: 213-836 7657

DOGLIGHT STUDIOS 226
TONY HONKAWA
600 Moulton Avenue #302
Los Angeles, California 90031
Tel. 213-222 1928

DORET, MICHAEL 227
12 East 14th Street #4-D
New York, NY 10003
Tel. 212-929 1688
    204 3738

EVENSON, STAN 228
4445 Overland Avenue
Culver City, California 90230
Tel. 213-204 1771
Fax: 213-204 4879

GERRIE, DEAN 229
515 North Main Street #210
Santa Ana, California 92701
Tel. 714-647 9488
Fax: 714-647 0193

GIRVIN, TIM 230-231
1601 Secord Avenue, 5th Floor
Seattle, Washington 98101
Tel. 206-623 7808
Fax: 206-340 1837

GRECO, PETER / LETTERING DESIGN 232
813 Westbourne Drive #7
West Hollywood, California 90069
Tel. 213-657 5085

HUME, KELLY 233
912 South Los Robles Avenue
Pasadena, California 91106
Tel. 818-793 8344

ISKRA LETTERING DESIGN 234-235
ISKRA JOHNSON
1605 12th Street #26
Seattle, Washington 98122
Tel. 206-323 8256

LARSON, RON 236
940 North Highland Avenue #E
Los Angeles, California 90038
Tel. 213-465 8451

BONNIE LEAH LETTERING & DESIGN 237
1801 Dove Street #104
Newport Beach, California 92660
Tel. 714-752 7820
Fax: 714-833 3367

LETTER•PERFECT 238
GARRET BOGE
6606 Soundview Drive
Gig Harbor, Washington 98335
Tel. 206-851 5158

MECHANICAL MEN, INC. 240
TRACY THOMAS
3958 Ince Boulevard
Culver City, California 90232
Tel. 213-837 1904
Fax: 213-837 0907

M SQUARED DESIGN 239
GLENNA WISEMAN
10559 Jefferson Boulevard
Culver City, California 90232
Tel. 213-202 0140
    213-202 0845
Fax: 213-202 8219

NIKOSEY, TOM 241
188 Dapplegray Road
Canoga Park
Bell Canyon, California 91307
Tel. 818-704 9993
Fax: 818-704 9995

OGLESBY ADVERTISING & DESIGN 242
CARLA OGLESBY
9520 Topanga Canyon Blvd. #100
Chatsworth, California 91311
Tel. 818-718 2012
Fax: 818-718 8241

PARSONS, GLENN 244
3958 Ince Boulevard
Culver City, California 90232
Tel. 213-559 6571

PATTERSON, MARK 243
OPTICAL ARTISTS
36 14th Street
Hermosa Beach, California 90254
Tel. 213-376 8859

ROMERO, JAVIER 245
9 West 19th Street, 5th Floor
New York, NY 10011
Tel. 212-727 9445
Fax: 212-727 3410

SCOPINICH, ROBERT 246
21026 Pacific Coast Highway
Malibu, California 90265
Tel. 213-456 7569

SIGWART, FORREST 247
1033 South Orlando Avenue
Los Angeles, California 90035
Tel. 213-655 7734
Fax: 213-655 2067

SPEAR, JEFFREY 248
2590 Centinela Avenue #7
Los Angeles, California 90064
Tel. 213-395 3939
Fax: 213-445 8935

STEVENS, JOHN 250-251
53 Clearmeadow Drive
East Meadow, NY 11554
Tel. 516-579 5352
Fax: 516-735 6535

30•SIXTY ADVERTISING & DESIGN, INC. 254-255
2801 Cahuenga Boulevard West
Los Angeles, California 90068
Tel. 213-850 5311

SHIFFMAN YOUNG DESIGN GROUP 249
7421 Beverly Boulevard #4
Los Angeles, California 90036
Tel. 213-930 1816

VIGON, JAY 252-253
11833 Brookdale Lane
Studio City, California 91604
Tel. 213-654 4771
    213-654 4996
Fax: 213-654 1915

Venezuela
Venezuela
Venezuela

MONTANA GRÁFICA DISEÑO 198-199
Av. Ppal. Boleíta Norte
Caracas 1060-A
Tel. 02-238 09 44
Fax: 02- 35 39 85

Designers

Hong Kong

Hongkong

Hong Kong

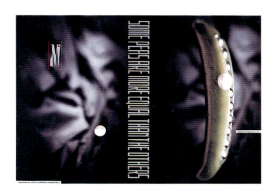

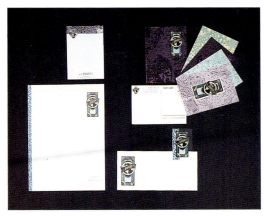

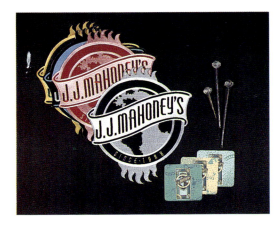

Regent Publishing Services...
western technology at eastern prices

We produce high quality books, magazines and brochures. We handle everything from four colour reproduction from transparencies and artwork, page assembly, printing and binding through to shipping, all at surprisingly competitive prices.

Production experts look after your jobs individually from our sales and production control centres in Hong Kong, New York and London.

Contact George, Albert or Gordon and ask for a quotation...

Hong Kong Office:
Call George Tai
REGENT PUBLISHING SERVICES LTD.
24TH FLOOR, FEDERAL CENTRE
77 SHEUNG ON STREET
CHAI WAN, HONG KONG,
Tel: 852-897-7803 Fax: 852-558-7209

New York Office:
Call Albert Yokum
REGENT PUBLISHING SERVICES LTD.
127 EAST 59TH STREET
NEW YORK, NY 10022, USA
Tel: 212-371-4506 Fax: 212-371-4609

London Office:
Call Gordon Beckwith
REGENT PUBLISHING SERVICES LTD.
4TH FLOOR, 4 BRANDON ROAD
LONDON N7 9TP, UK
Tel: 071-607-3322 Fax: 071-700-4985

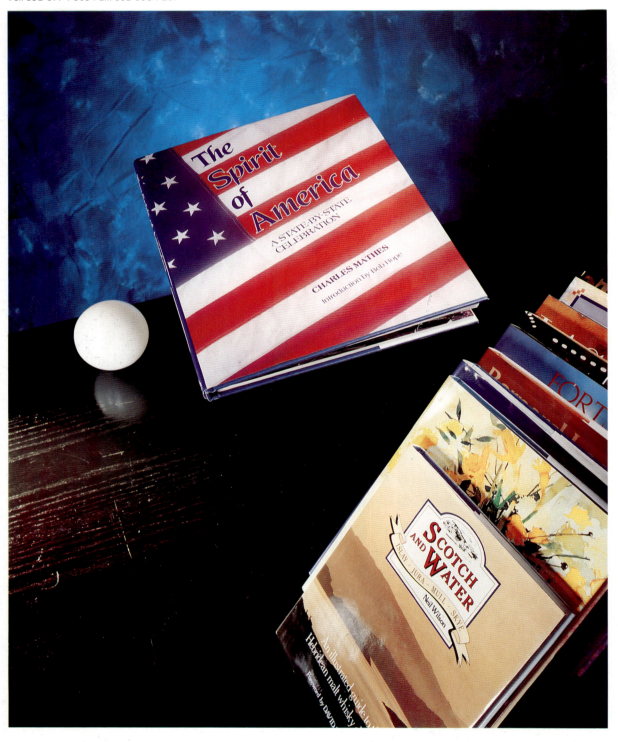

Designers

Korea
Corée
Korea

SEOUL GRAPHIC CENTER

The 5th., Seoul Graphic Center Bldg., 436-11, Chang-jeon Dong, Ma-po ku, Seoul 121-00. Korea. Tel. 324-5402, 336-3074. Fax : 332-6706.

Korea Electric Power Corporation (1985)

Dong Hwa Bank (1989)

Kolon Group (1981)

Hannam Chemical Corporation (1979)

Munhwa Broadcasting Corporation (1986)

Dong Ah Group (1979)

Lotte Chilsung Beverage Co., Ltd. (1986)

La Sposa (1985)

Cho Hung Bank (1986)

Cygnus Time Inc. (1988)

Ssangyong Group (1977)

Daewoong Pharmaceutical Co., Ltd. (1978)

Bowon Trading Co., Ltd. (1987)

Kukdong Oil Company Ltd. (1989)

Shindongah Group (1989)

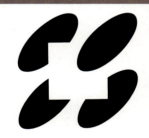

Hanil Feed Mill Ind. Co., Ltd. (A tentative Plan) (1990)

Taegeuk (A tentative Plan for '88 Seoul Olympic Games) (1988)

Dong Hwa Bank (A tentative Plan) (1989)

Daelim Trading Co., Ltd. (1981)

Shindongah Group (A tentative Plan) (1989)

Creative Director......Kwon Myung Kwang
Research and Planner......Oh Kun Jae
Art Director......Moon Chul
Chief Designer......Suh Hong Sun
Graphic Designer......Kim Joo Sung
Graphic Designer......Moon Hong Jin
Graphic Designer......Kim Chang Seek

Graphic Designer......Kim Sae Hoon
Graphic Designer......Park In Chang
Graphic Designer......Park Hae Young
Industrial Designer......Kim Sung Bu
Fashion Designer......Kim Hae Ja
Assistant......Lee Hong Ja

564 SHINSA-DONG, KANGNAM-KU, SEOUL, KOREA   PHONE (02) 512-2283, 2284, 2285   FAX (02) 512-2286   ■ CORPORATE IDENTIFICATION PROGRAM   ■ IMAGE ANALYSIS

DESIGN
BRIDGE

32F. Korea World Trade Center
159-1 Samsungdong Kangnamku
Seoul Korea 135-729
Phone 02-551-3271
Fax 02-551-3275

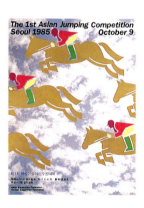

ALL COMMUNICATIONS

Art for Life and Love

1. Ministry of Communications
2. Seoul Arts Center
3. Yosu Energy (L. P. Gas Producing & Distributing Company.)
4. Korea First Bank
5. Bank of Korea
6. Cheil Sugar & Co., Ltd. (Foods Manufacturer)
7. Pusan Bank
8. Kyongnam Bank
9. Hyundai Electronics
10. Bank of Seoul

3

1

2

4

5

6

7

8

9

Following on the outstanding success with its initial project for Korea First Bank in 1980, ALL (Art for Life & Love) Communications, now fondly called ALLcom by its ever lengthening list of clients, quickly emerged as an invincible force in Korea's CI market.
With many of its research and working-level staffs as modest, quiet-talking college professors, ALL Communications, instead of the usual format of oral presentation, has adopted the method of slide sessions to convince its clients of what is best for them, who, in their turn, never fail to appreciate what a bona fide CI project means and what it could do for them when conducted properly.

10

ALL COMMUNICATIONS

Art for
Life and
Love

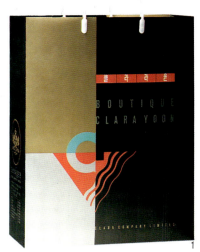

1. Boutique Clara (High-Fashion Dress Shop)
2. Seoul Land (Amusement Park)
3. Myeong Dong Catholic Cathedral
4. Citizens Investment Trust Management Co., Ltd.
5. Crown Beer
6. Grandjoie (Sparkling Wine)
7. Cheil Frozen Foods
8. Barunson (Fancy Goods Manufacturer)
9. Cheil Genetic Engineering & Co., Ltd.
10. Hyundae Sheet
11. Korea Management Association

All Communications
Red House 3, 4 FL., 721 Banpo-dong, Seocho-gu, Seoul, Korea
Tel.: 02-549·6440, 6441 Fax.: 02-549·6441

HEXA INTERNATIONAL
TOTAL DESIGN SERVICE

Phone (02) 733-0445
Fax (02) 737-7704
Modem (02) 733-0446
208-18, Buam-dong Jongro-gu
Seoul 110-021, Korea

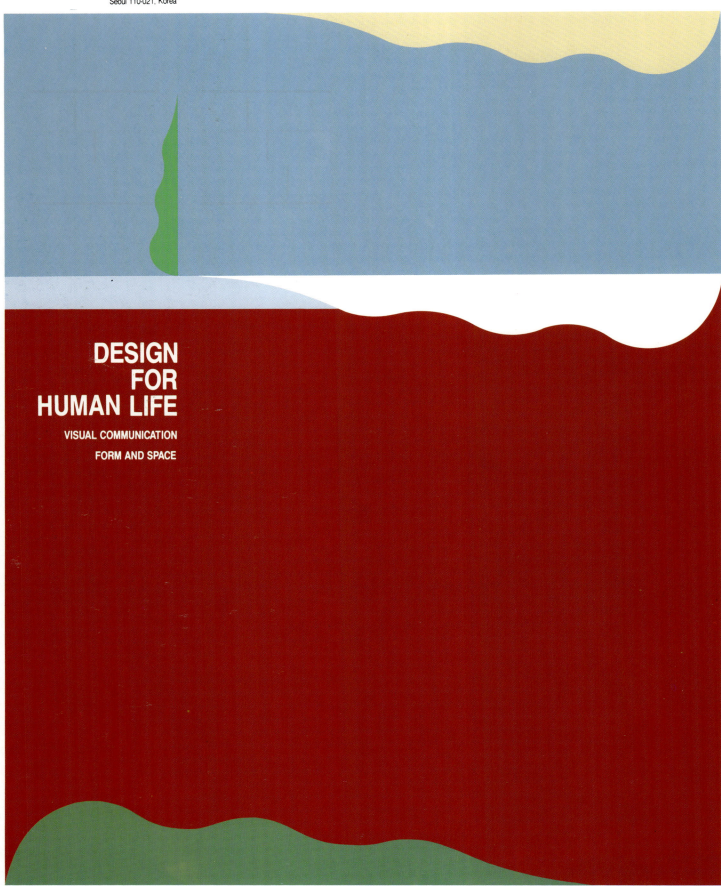

**DESIGN
FOR
HUMAN LIFE**

VISUAL COMMUNICATION

FORM AND SPACE

KIM JAE-HYUN

Hosan Bldg, 2F
709-8, Banpo-Dong
Seocho-ku
Seoul 137 040
Korea
Tel. 02-512 3948
      512 3949
Fax : 02-512 3948

Agent :
Cross Cultural Center for Asia
Hosan Bldg, 2F
709-8, Banpo-Dong
Seocho-ku
Seoul 137 040
Korea

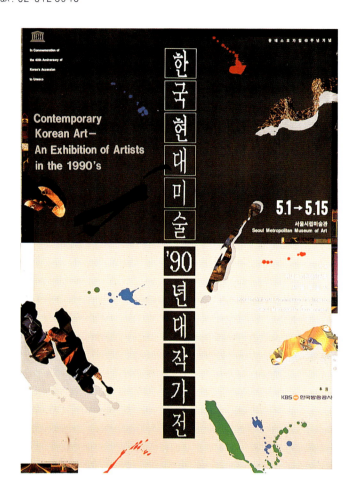

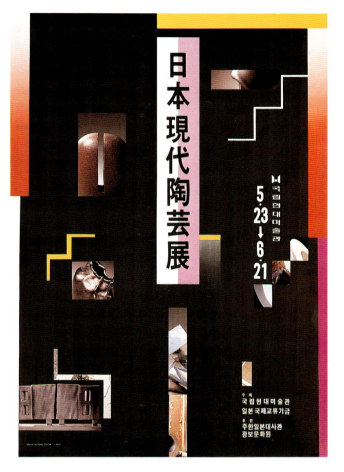

SEOUL
DESIGN CENTER

SEOUL DESIGN CENTER
4F MOON HWA BLDG, 47-15, 2-KA, JEO-DONG, CHOONG-KU, SEOUL, KOREA
TEL. 272-8646~7. FAX. 278-8771

Specialized in drawing package design, SEOUL DESIGN CENTER maintaining a close relationship with those who are engaged in commodity production, development and sales activities in pursuit of maximized profit, is providing them with ideas of how to improve package design of their commodities.

SEOUL
DESIGN CENTER

SEOUL DESIGN CENTER

4F MOON HWA BLDG, 47-15, 2-KA, JEO-DONG, CHOONG-KU, SEOUL, KOREA
TEL. 272-8646~7. FAX. 278-8771

Specialized in drawing package design, SEOUL DESIGN CENTER maintaining a close relationship with those who are engaged in commodity production, development and sales activities in pursuit of maximized profit, is providing them with ideas o how to improve package design of their commodities.

ahn graphicS ltd.

1-34 Tongsung-dong, Chongno-gu, Seoul 110-510, Korea
Phone: (02) 743-8065/6, 4154, 763-2320
Fax.: (02) 744-3251 Modem: 745-7209
Electronic Mail: ahn01dh CompuServe: 72401, 1230

Poster for the quarterly magazine
Pogosŏ / Pogosŏ

ahn graphics ltd.

1-34 Tongsung-dong, Chongno-gu, Seoul 110-510, Korea
Phone: (02) 743-8065/6, 4154, 763-2320
Fax.: (02) 744-3251 Modem: 745-7209
Electronic Mail: ahn01dh CompuServe: 72401, 1230

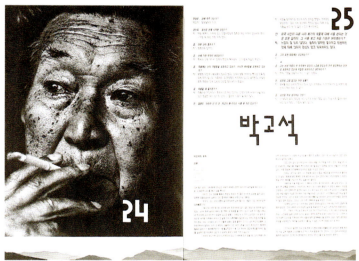

Spread from the quarterly magazine *Pogosŏ/Pogosŏ*

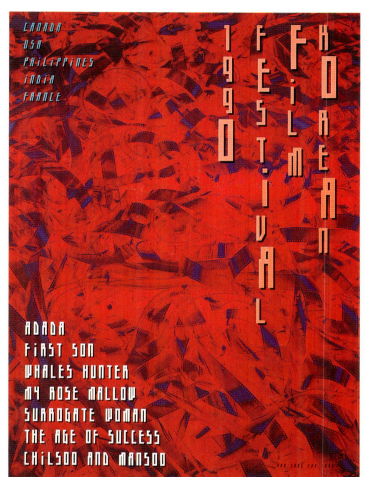

Poster for the Korean Film Festival

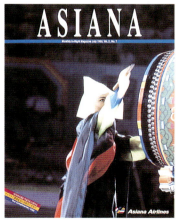

Cover for *Asiana*, the in-flight magazine of
Asiana Airlines

Cover for the Buddhist Broadcasting System's
corporate image manual

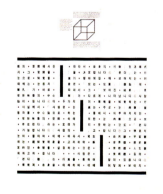
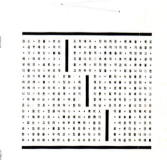

Spread from a pamphlet for a private exhibit

C D R

CDR, INC.
666-5, Yoksam-dong,
Kangnam-ku, Seoul, KOREA
Tel: (001-82-2) 557-3353, 3354
Fax: (001-82-2) 557-5880

Namsung Corp.

Shinsegae Department Store
Co., Ltd.

Daelim Industrial Co., Ltd.

Chungbuk Bank

The Citizens National Bank

Peeres Cosmetics Ltd.

Korea Long Term Credit Bank

A & M Metals Inc.

Samlip Foods Industrial Co., Ltd

Korea Merchant Banking Co.

Mascot for the Citizens
National Bank

KIA Motors Corp.

Korea Investment Trust Co., Ltd.

Pohang Institute of Science &
Technology

Dong-A Pharmaceutical Co.,
Ltd.

Dongsuh Foods Corp.

Korea Exchange Bank

Mascot for Daewoo Securities
Co., Ltd.

KEDIA Incorporation

Eagon Industrial Co., Ltd.

Cheil Synthetic Textiles Co., Ltd

Fashion Institute of Kolon

Oriental Brewery Co., Ltd.

Daehan Kyoyuk Life Insurance
Co., Ltd.

Korea Foreign Trade
Association

Riverside Hotel

The Korea Development Bank

OB Super Dry Beer

Lucky Ltd.

Cheil Sugar Co., Ltd.

Korea Kyowon Univ.

Cheil Wool Textile Co., Ltd.

C D R

CORPORATE
IDENTITY AND
PACKAGING

Symbol mark for Daelim Industrial Co., Ltd.

Application on vehicle for Daelim Industrial Co., Ltd.

Symbol mark for Eagon Industrial Co., Ltd.

Application on vehicle for Eagon Industrial Co., Ltd.

Sign application for KIA Motors Corp.

Standing sign for KIA Motors Corp.

Application on vehicle for KIA Motors Corp.

Symbol mark for Namsung Corp.

Symbol mark for Peeres Cosmetics Ltd.

Application on vehicle for Peeres Cosmetics Ltd.

Package for Peeres Cosmetics Ltd.

Symbol mark for Samlip Foods Industrial Co., Ltd.

Symbol mark for Shinsegae Department Store Co., Ltd.

Standing sign for Dong-A Pharmaceutical Co., Ltd.

Application on vehicle for Dong-A Pharmaceutical Co., Ltd.

Package for Dong-A Pharmaceutical Co., Ltd.

Corporate flag for Korea Exchange Bank

Display sign for Korea Exchange Bank

Symbol mark for Korea Investment Trust Co., Ltd.

Standing sign for Korea Investment Trust Co., Ltd.

Standing sign for Korea Long Term Credit Bank

Letterheads application for Korea Long Term Credit Bank

Symbol mark for Chungbuk Bank

Standing sign for Chungbuk Bank

Sign application for Fashion Institute of Kolon

Label for OB Super Dry Beer

OB bottle label

OB can label

Package for Crown Electronics Co., Ltd.

Symbol mark for Lucky Ltd.

Application on vehicle for Lucky Ltd.

Standing sign for Dongnam Securities Co., Ltd.

Corporate flag for the Citizens National Bank

Cigarette package for the Citizens National Bank

Symbol mark for Dongsuh Foods Corp.

Package for Dongsuh Foods Corp.

Mascot for Daewoo Securities Co., Ltd.

Package for Cheil Sugar Co., Ltd.

Application on drinking glasses for Riverside Hotel

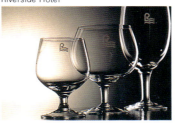

Symbol mark for KEDIA Inc.

C D R

POSTER DESIGN

Official Poster for the 1988 Seoul Olympics

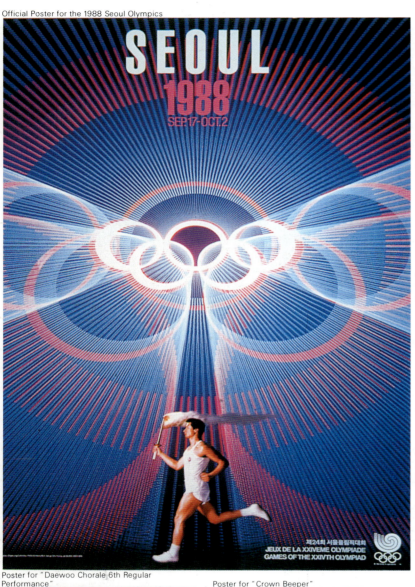

1988 Seoul Olympic Sports Poster ‹Rowing›

1988 Seoul Olympic Sports Poster ‹Archery›

1988 Seoul Olympic Sports Poster ‹Table Tennis›

1988 Seoul Olympic Sports Poster ‹Equestrian Sports›

1988 Seoul Olympic Sports Poster ‹Athletics›

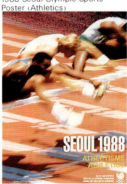

1988 Seoul Olympic Sports Poster ‹Shooting›

Poster for "Daewoo Chorale 6th Regular Performance"

Poster for "Crown Beeper"

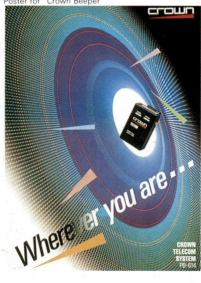

Cover design for IDEA magazine.

The INFINITE GROUP is a recognized leader in the field of marketing communications and strategic design. The firm places special emphasis on using multifaceted approach to the application of design in assessing a client's visual identity needs. This system involves the total integration of marketing management with corporate, branding, retail and signing identities. The INFINITE GROUP has designed a wide and dynamic range of important and successful identity programs for some of the leading korean and international corporations, hotels and institutions. The firm has a multi-lingual staff who have extensive experience in their respective field of expertise as well as a diversified international network of design and marketing consultants. To every project the INFINITE GROUP brings the same basic philosophy that design is the coherent visual extension of a company's marketing activities.

12F. Anguk Bldg. 175-87, Anguk-Dong, Chongro-Gu, Seoul, Korea.

Fax: 737-6907, Tel: 736-7533 ~ 5

INFINITE GROUP
Identity Management Consultants

12F, Anguk Bldg.
175-87, Anguk-Dong, Chongro-Gu, Seoul, Korea
Tel: 736-7533 ~ 5, Fax: 737-6907

Cheju Shilla Hotel

Korean Racing Association

Seven Summits Resort

Korean Tourist Office

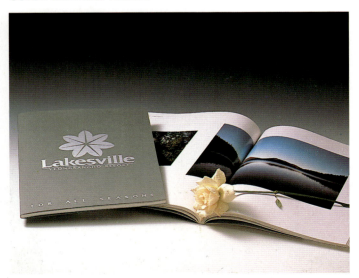

Lakesville Resort

Samho Foods

I N F I N I T E G R O U P

Identity Management Consultants

12F, Anguk Bldg.
175-87, Anguk-Dong, Chongro-Gu, Seoul, Korea
Tel: 736-7533 ~ 5, Fax: 737-6907

Kisan Corporation

Cacatoa Childrens Fashion

Samhorang Fastfood Chain

Chungmun Beach Golf & Country

Samsung General Chemicals

Raiders Pro Baseball Team

43

Identity Management Consultants

Corporate Identity System

Brand Identity System

Signage System

Name Creation & Nomenclature System

Marketing Research & Strategic Planning

Trademark Search System

Client List

Cheju Shilla Hotel

Seven Summits Muju Resort

Ssang Bang Wool Raiders Pro Baseball Team

Lakesville Resort

Samho Foods Corporation

Yeonhap Insu Corporation

Kumho Group

Kisan Construction

Korea National Tourist Office

Korean Racing Association

Hanil Group

Hyundai Motors

Ssang Bang Wool Corporation

Samsung General Chemicals

Dae Kyung Foods Corporation

Hansaem Publishing Co.

Cheil Foods Corporation

IBM Korea

Hyatt International

Jindo Corporation

Seoul Foreign Clinic

Dong Jin Construction

12F. Anguk Bldg. 175-87, Anguk-Dong, Chongro-Gu, Seoul, Korea.

Fax: 737-6907. Tel: 736-7533 ~ 5

Designers

Indonesia
Indonésie
Indonesien

PHOTOGRAPHED BY

ALOYSIUS ADJI WATONO

46

DWI SAPTA PRATAMA
ADVERTISING

OFFICE: Kelapa Gading Boulevard TN 2/23 Kelapa Gading Permai, Jakarta 14240. Telp.: 4511675, 4710814. Starko: 3802701, 361101, α 10327

STUDIO: Jl. Ekor Kuning III/27 Rawamangun, Jakarta 13220 Telp.: 4894665, 4712207. Fax: 4890292

PHOTOGRAPHED BY

ALOYSIUS ADJI WATONO

47

GUA GRAPHIC

PT. GAJAH UTAMA AGUNG

JL.SALEMBARAYA I/20 JAKARTA 10430

TEL. (021) 331160 , 333993. FAX. (021) 333990

PO.BOX. 83/KBYTB JAKARTA 12001

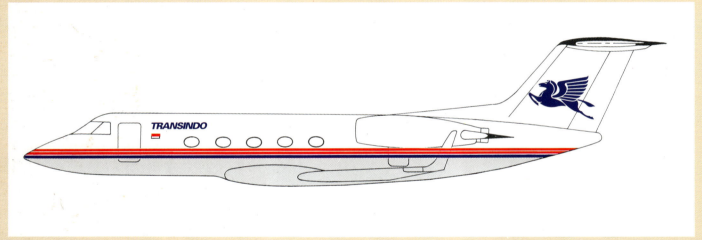

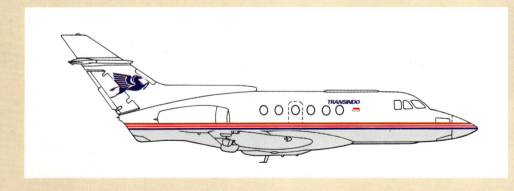

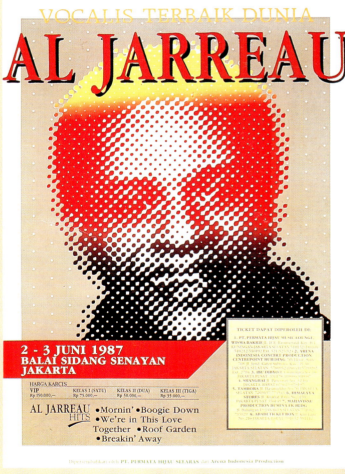

graphic house

JAZZ FESTIVAL

ILLUSTRATION

Packaging
Window Display
Greeting Cards

PT. PROSPEK DIMENSIGRAFIK
Jl. Bumi Kemanggisan IV
Blok D 1, Jakarta 11480
TEL. 5493509

AU GRAPHIC DESIGN

Represented by

Saka Infosa
SENTRA KREASI

Jl. Ciasem IV/24
Kebayoran Baru, Jakarta Selatan
Tel. (021) 717038   Fax. (021) 770284
INDONESIA

SiAga

SiAga stands for **Simpanan Keluarga**, a family savings-account product issued by BANK BUKOPIN, the **Cooperative Bank** of Indonesia

GUGUS GRAFIS

GRAPHIC COMMUNICATION DESIGN

JL. PEJOMPONGAN RAYA NO. 23
PO. BOX 35 / JKPPJ JAKARTA 10210
PHONE 581373 - 583562. FAX 581373.

PACKAGING DESIGN
CORPORATE COMMUNICATION DESIGN
PUBLICATION DESIGN
PROMOTION DESIGN

Designers

Malaysia

Malaisie

Malaysia

FGA
FIXGO ADVERTISING (M) SDN BHD

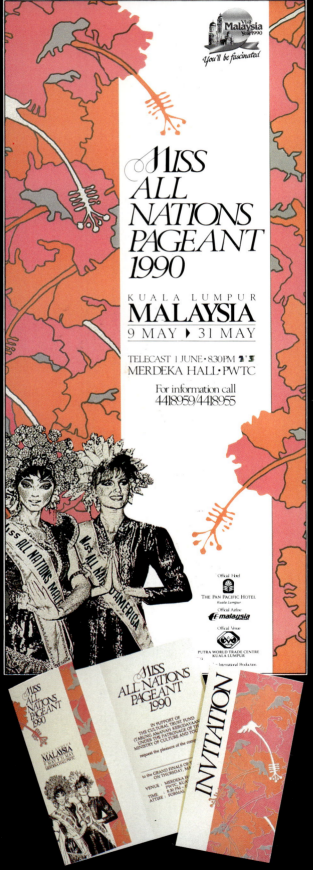

A Little Luxury

As mild as cleansing cream, yet as clean as soap and water. Dermatologically proven gentle enough for all facial skin types. Cleanses without stripping off your skin's natural oils.

Liquid Neutrogena®

Pure Protection

For the active who constantly expose their skin to the harmful rays of the sun, there's Neutrogena Moisture SPF 15 (untinted). A moisturiser that keeps skin well-hydrated and yet gives the added protection and safety of a PABA free SPF 15 sunscreen.

Neutrogena® Moisture SPF 15

CREATIVE DIRECTION ▼ ALLEN TAN   PHOTOGRAPHY ▼ FOUR FIVE STUDIO   COLOR SEPARATION ▼ KLIM LITHO

28, 2nd FLOOR, JALAN SS19/1D
SUBANG JAYA, 47500 PETALING JAYA
SELANGOR, MALAYSIA.
TEL: 03-7336596 FAX: 03-733-1857

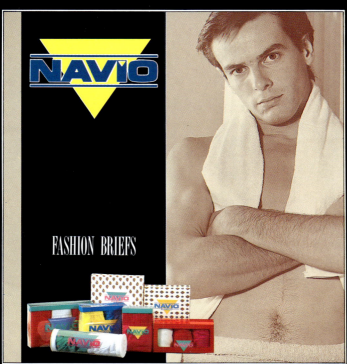

NAVIO MEN'S BRIEFS POSTER

BERGER PAINTS CALENDAR

S'FARE PRESS AD

WALT DISNEY STATIONERY

PACKAGING & CATALOGUES FROM CAELYGIRL

No 21A SS 21/37 Damansara Utama
47400 Petaling Jaya Selangor
Tel: 03-7193000 03-7172875
Fax: 603-7172875

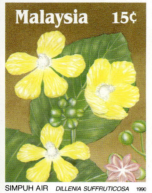

Malaysia 15¢

SIMPUH AIR *DILLENIA SUFFRUTICOSA* 1990

Malaysia 20¢

PUTERI MALU *MIMOSA PUDICA* 1990

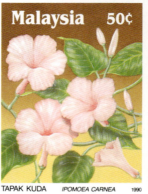

Malaysia 50¢

TAPAK KUDA *IPOMOEA CARNEA* 1990

Malaysia $1

TELEPOK *NYMPHAEA PUBESCENS* 1990

SETEM POS KHAS
Special Issue of Postage Stamps

BUNGA-BUNGA LIAR
WILD FLOWERS OF
Malaysia

BUTIRAN TEKNIK

Tarikh Keluaran: 12hb. Mac, 1990
Denominasi: 15 sen, 20 sen, 50 sen dan 1 ringgit
Saiz Setem: 28mm x 39mm
Kertas: Tera air SPM, bersalut fosfor
Proses Percetakan: Litograf
Pencetak: Security Printers (M) Sdn. Bhd,
46050 Petaling Jaya, Malaysia.
Kandungan Sehelai: 100 Setem
Perekabentuk Setem: Tony Teh Chin Seng c/o De Art Forms Sdn. Bhd.

Setem-setem ini adalah dalam warna penuh dan akan di jual dari 12hb.
Mac, 1990 selama enam bulan atau sehingga stok habis, yang mana
terlebih dahulu.

TECHNICAL DETAILS

Date of Issue: 12th March, 1990
Denomination: 15¢, 20¢, 50¢ and $1
Stamp Size: 28mm x 39mm
Paper: SPM Watermarked phosphor coated
Printing Process: Lithography
Printer: Security Printers (M) Sdn. Bhd,
46050 Petaling Jaya, Malaysia.
Sheet Content: 100 stamps
Stamp Designer: Tony Teh Chin Seng c/o De Art Forms Sdn. Bhd.

The stamps are in full colour and will be on sale from 12th March, 1990
for a period of six months or until stocks are exhausted, whichever is
the earlier.

Pek Cenderamata berharga $2.50 tiap-tiap satu dan Kad
Setem (Maximum Card) berharga $1.00 (4 kad satu set)
akan dijual dari 12hb Mac, 1990 sehingga stok habis.

Presentation Pack costing $2.50 each and Post Office
Stamp Card (Maximum Card) costing $1.00 (per set of 4)
will be on sale from 12th March, 1990 until stocks are
exhausted.

UNTUK KETERANGAN LANJUT TENTANG
PENGENDALIAN AKAUN PESANAN TETAP DAN
MAKLUMAT YANG LAIN TENTANG SETEM SILA
HUBUNGI:

FOR DETAILS OF OPERATING A STANDING ORDER
ACCOUNT AND ANY OTHER INFORMATION REGARDING
STAMPS PLEASE CONTACT:

Ketua Pengarah Pos, (Biro Peminat Setem),
Tingkat Satu, Pejabat Pos Besar, Kompleks Dayabumi,
50670 Kuala Lumpur. Tel: 03-2741122 (Samb. 1189/1063)

Improving your complexion is no longer a gamble

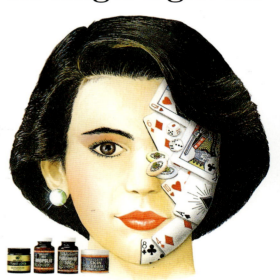

Your skin is a complex creation of Nature. What better way to care for your skin than with Nature's best.

High-Desert products, for a beautiful complexion, contain Nature's very best ingredients — honeybee pollen, royal jelly and bee propolis. They help your complexion glow and radiate health in a thoroughly natural manner.

Take the wise way to healthier skin. The High-Desert way — it's a sure bet!

MONEY-BACK Assurance
High-Desert is so sure of its products that it also offers a money-back programme to those who qualify. Many have tried and found the products effective, and have volunteered their testimonials and photos.

Professional facials also available:
Highly experienced (and gentle) High-Desert Beauty Therapists are in the P. J. head-office should you need their advice or service.
Come for a FREE skin analysis with no obligation to buy.

Come for a free demo & slide show to find out more! Call 03-7750908

HIGH-DESERT (M) Sdn Bhd
(Head-office): 181 Jalan SS 2/24, 47300 Petaling Jaya.
Excellent products from the cool mountainous deserts of Arizona, U.S.A.

Yes! I am interested to know more about High-Desert products. Name: _____
Address: _____
Send this coupon to Customer Service Dept. 181 Jalan SS 2/24, 47300 Petaling Jaya. Thank you.

Branches in Malaysia:

Alor Setar 04-710 572	Kuala Kangsar 05-865 733	Melaka 06-241 240
Butterworth 04-304 641	Kota Bahru 09-745 115	Seremban 06-728 880
Ipoh 05-506096/509819	Kota Kinabalu 088-212 236	Taiping 05-826 287
Johor Bahru 07-240 863	Kuantan 09-514 098	
Kuala Lumpur 03-241 6389	Kuching 082-413 735	Singapore office 02-235 5656

Colour Separation by Phans Graphic Tel: 03-7919321. Fax: 603-7918906.

ONE • STOP CREATIVE BOOK

CENTRE

CREATIVE BOOKS FOR ADVERTISING & DESIGN •

FLO

ENTERPRISE SDN. BHD.

42-A JALAN SS 21/58
DAMANSARA UTAMA
47400 PETALING JAYA
SELANGOR, MALAYSIA
TEL: 03-7187770/90
FAX: 7186426

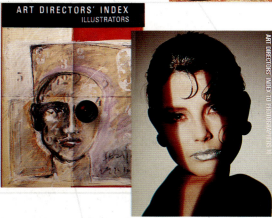

DESIGNER • KS YUEN • DESIGN • SKY

Designers

Singapore

Singapour

Singapur

FIE–JJA 60

BOOK COVER
ROTOVISION SA
SWITZERLAND

WORSHIP MUSIC MINISTRY

GSN INTERNATIONAL
TELEVISION PTE LTD

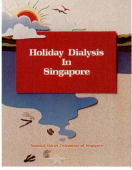

BROCHURE DESIGN
NATIONAL KIDNEY
FOUNDATION

CORPORATE BROCHURE
FORBES MANAGEMENT
CONSULTANTS

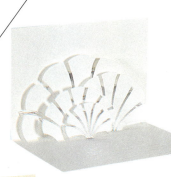

ROYAL WEDDING
SAUDI ARABIA

BIRTHDAY CARD
PRUDENTIAL
ASSURANCE
COMPANY LTD

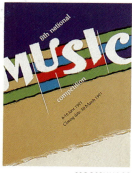

PROGRAMME BOOKLET
MINISTRY OF
COMMUNITY
DEVELOPMENT

CHRISTMAS CARD
NATIONAL
KIDNEY
FOUNDATION

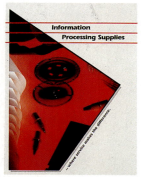

MEDIA SUPPLY CATALOGUE
INSING TAI ENTERPRISE
PRIVATE LIMITED

fie-jja

fie-jja
111 north bridge road
suite 05-24
peninsula plaza
singapore 0617

tel: 065-3396 795
fax: 065-3370 024

creative consultant
priscilla teoh

— 3-dimensional card,
  menu, calendar &
  promotional item.

— corporate identity

— publication

Colour Separation by Columbia Offset Group

Designers

Thailand
Thaïlande
Thailand

COMPUTER GRAPHIC

Design

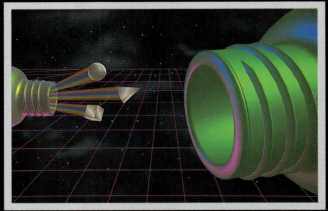

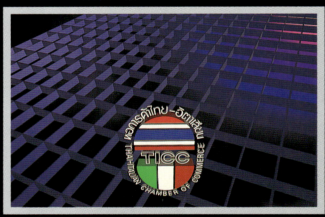

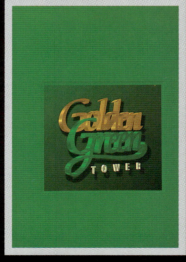

Vision Innovation

1044/4 SUKHUMVIT 44/2   BANGKOK 10110 TEL. 392-3525

CompuProductions

CompuProductions is the South East Asia leader in the implementation of Macintosh Graphic Solutions for the Advertising and Marketing industries.

Photography - 35mm, 6x7cm, 4x5"
Image Scanning - transparencies and flat art
Image Manipulation - retouching, special effects
Animation - product simulation, information kiosks, inter-active multi-media presentations
Film Recording - from computer to film, 35mm, 4x5"; computer graphics and manipulated scans
Slide Presentations - 35mm, text, charts, graphics
Computer Presentations - boardroom, ballroom or discoteque; images that move
Video Production - S-VHS and U-Matic for training, product promotion and marketing
Events Production - product launch, seminars, conventions, birthday parties and weddings
Computer System Consulting - publishing and graphics systems for advertising industry and in-house publishing departments

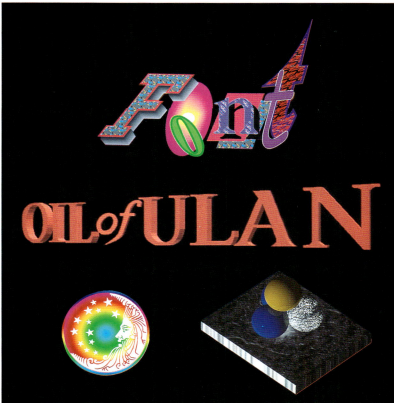

CompuPrint is the South East Asia leader in the implementation of Macintosh Typesetting and Layout Solutions for the Publishing, Advertising and Marketing industries.

Brochures - travel, real estate, manufactured goods
Business Cards - laser and off-set
Letterheads - your design or new logo created
Proposals - high quality and strictest confidence
Financial Reports - clean and easy to understand
Annual Reports - we produce the best
Project Reports - VOLAGs and private industry
Menus - restaurants and hotels
Posters - travel, entertainment, hotels
Tent Cards - hotels, restaurants
Album Covers - local and international market
Catalogues - export, wholesale, retail
Books - paperbacks, travel, art
Newsletters - VOLAGs, corporations

Anything that requires page layout

Fourth Floor, 3 Patpong 1
Silom Rd., Bangrak
Bangkok, Thailand 10500
Tel: 236-4976-8 Fax: 236-4979

CompuPrint

Designers

Belgium
Belgique
Belgien

CATEGORIES	DECOBO	DELTA DESIGN	HERMANN	PINEAPPLE	STRUYF & PARTNERS
2 – DIMENSIONAL					
Art Direction			●		●
Computer Graphic				●	
Corporate Design			●	●	
Graphic Design		●	●	●	●
Packaging Design		●		●	●
3 – DIMENSIONAL					
Display Design					
Environmental Design					
Industrial Design		●			
Interior Design	●				
Product Design					
Textile Design					

PINEAPPLE DESIGN S.A.

Rue de la Consolation 56 Troostraat
Bruxelles 1030 Brussels
Belgium
Tel. 02-242 78 20
Fax: 02-242 96 40

PINEAPPLE DESIGN S.A. is a design consultancy specialising in package design, brand development and corporate identity design.

PINEAPPLE DESIGN S.A. est une agence-conseil en design, spécialisée en packaging, développement de marque et visage d'entreprises.

PINEAPPLE DESIGN S.A. ist eine Designer-Beratungsagentur, spezialisiert in Verpackungs-Design, Marken-Entwicklung und Corporate Identity Design.

PINEAPPLE DESIGN

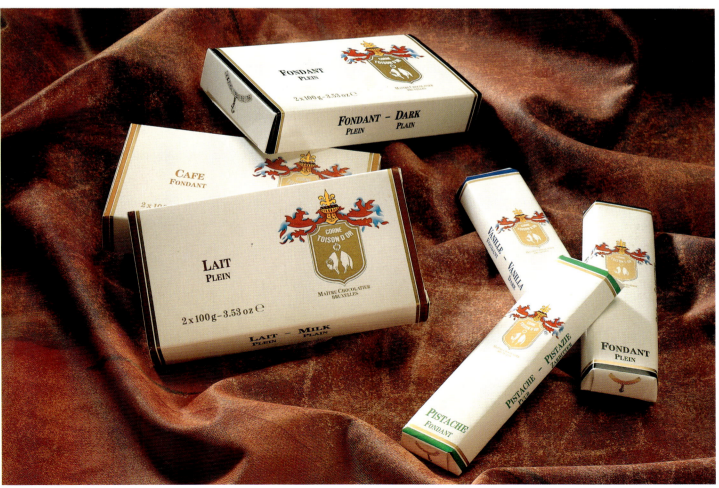

HERMANN ADVERTISING

Kolonel Begaultlaan 15 / 3
B-3012 Leuven – Brussels
Tel. 32-16-22 24 91
Fax : 32-16-29 24 96

Art Director :
Herman Vanaerschot

Agent in UK :
Michael Rynne (Device) London
Unit 8 – A. Davis Industrial Estate
Somerlayton Road – London SW9 8ND
Tel. 44-71-737 3983
Agent in Germany : Eveline Varga
Sinkenweg 7
D-6057 Dietzenbach 1 Frankfurt
Tel. 49-6074-31807

Consulting and full service for advertising, promotion and graphic design. Our approach of people and their commercial environment results in strong graphic design, expressive photography and remarkably better sales results.

Advies en full-service bureau voor advertising, promotie en grafisch design. Onze benadering van mensen en hun commerciële omgeving resulteert in sterk grafisch design, karaktervolle fotografie en opmerkelijk betere verkoopsresultaten.

PEPSI COLA   *calendar*

INTERBREW   *international promotion*

MESSERSCHMITT   *Me 109 early morning juin 30 1990*

DECOBO

EDDY CORBEEL

Hovenierstraat 39
B-2800 Mechelen
Tel. +32-15-42 15 50
Fax : +32-15-42 29 06

Interior design for offices, shops and hotels.
DECOBO realisations are the logical result of a client oriented, functional approach to space and design.

Interieur design voor kantoor-winkel-hotel.
DECOBO realisaties zijn het logisch gevolg van een klantgerichte en funktionele aanpak van ruimten en design.

Architecture d'intérieur pour bureaux, magasins et hôtels.
Les créations DECOBO sont l'aboutissement logique d'une approche fonctionnelle de l'espace et du graphisme au service du client.

INTERIOR DESIGN

DECOBO

& BUILDING

DELTADESIGN INT. ASSOCIATES S.P.R.L. B.V.B.A.

Consultant:
Bruno Anquinel
Nadine Tasquin
Madeliefjesstraat 48
B-1850 Grimbergen
Tel. 02-269 59 83
Fax : 02-269 76 24

DELTADESIGN: top package designer.
Trade marks and its applications;
product innovation; conception of
promotions of all kinds; production;
market studies.

DELTADESIGN: à la pointe du
graphisme, packaging design.
Image de marque et leurs applications;
innovation de produit; conception de
promotion en tous genres; production;
étude de marché.

DELTA DESIGN
Associates

Designers

Holland

Hollande

Holland

CATEGORIES	BOZELL	CLAESSENS	H. & E. ELBERS	KOPERDRAAD	A. MAES	MILLFORD/ VAN DEN BERG	SAMENWERKENDE ONTWERPERS	STEMPELS & OSTER	VAN VELSEN
2 – DIMENSIONAL									
Art Direction			●			●	●		
Computer Graphic								●	
Corporate Design		●	●		●			●	
Graphic Design	●		●			●		●	
Packaging Design	●	●	●		●		●		
3 – DIMENSIONAL									
Display Design	●								
Environmental Design	●			●					
Industrial Design	●			●					
Interior Design	●	●		●		●			
Product Design		●		●			●		
Textile Design				●					

SO

AJAX

Samenwerkende Ontwerpers (SO Design)
2- and 3-dimensional design, was founded in Amsterdam in 1983. Always, the standards of SO Design imply that the translation of the message must involve more than what was strictly formulated in advance. This manner of working has led to growing interest and appreciation, both nationally and internationally.

Samenwerkende Ontwerpers (SO Design)
2- and 3-dimensional design
Herengracht 160
1016 BN Amsterdam
The Netherlands
Telephone 31(0)20-6 24 05 47
Telefax 31(0)20-6 23 53 09
For information contact:
Marianne Vos or André Toet

Ajax • A new corporate identity, sign system (new stadium) for the Amsterdam based football club Ajax. SO is probably the first Dutch agency involved in such a project.

Mart. Spruijt • For one of the best printers in the Netherlands, Mart. Spruijt Printers, we designed a house style. Not purely typographic, no new 'synoptic' logotype, but an impression of a printing house.

Volksbuurtmuseum • Logotype and housestyle for the still to be built 'Working Class Quarter Museum' (Volksbuurtmuseum) in The Hague.

Dagbladunie • Situated at the head-office of Dagbladunie (the major newspaper publisher in the Netherlands) we placed this sign (as part of the new corporate identity) more an eyecatcher than an example of conventional architectural lettering.

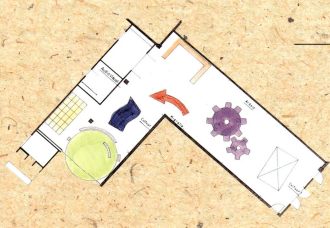

Volksbuurtmuseum • Exhibition design is a very important part of our practice. At the moment we are designing the permanent exhibition of the 'Working Class Quarter Museum' (Volksbuurtmuseum). It is scheduled to open in Spring 1992.

Malevich catalogue • Packaging, Bags or Wrapping paper are common jobs at SO. This is a packaging for special clients of Dagbladunie, who received a catalogue of the Russian painter Kasimir Malevich.

'Kunst bewegt die Könige und bringt die Esel zum fliegen' *Sandro Chia 1988*

»WHAT GOOD IS THE BEAUTY OF YOUR PACKAGING WHEN IT ONLY ATTRACTS DUST ON THE SHELVES?«

A new approach by René de Witte, managing director Claessens Product Consultants.

It so happens sometimes that even professional marketing people mistake beauty for effectiveness, when packaging design is concerned. When thinking about packaging one can really say, that there is more than meets the eye. In fact it is the only Permanent Medium amongst all marketing tools. It is on the shelves that the final battle for the consumers' preference takes place. Hence, the name of the game is Effectiveness. If and when that goal can be reached by "beauty" all the better. But that is not our prime criterion.

PRODUCT, BRAND AND PERSONALITY THE UNDIVISIBLE THREESOME.

New products are being launched. Virtually every day. The Marketing Company, without fail, pays full attention to all financial, juridical

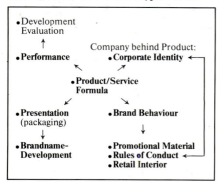

and industrial aspects. In this merry-go-round of events too often the value of the undivisible threesome is underestimated…
The creation of a brand is being endangered, the building of a personality is way off.

INVITATION FOR AN INDIVIDUAL* ONE-DAY SEMINAR IN HILVERSUM, HOLLAND.

At the occasion of our organisation's 30th anniversary we have pleasure in inviting you for an individual one-day seminar on the above mentioned subjects. Purpose of the exercise is to replace confusion by coherence as far as the development of brands and personalities through packaging is concerned. Obviously, your participation is free of charge (you may consider it as our birthday present to you without any string attached). Since we are very much in favour of open discussions we have chosen for the individual formula.

* a limited number of representatives from one company at the time

PROGRAMME

09.00 h. Welcome. Coffee. Introduction by one of our senior consultants
09.45 h. Analyses
10.30 h. Coffee
10.45 h. Communication targets
11.15 h. Non-verbal communication
12.00 h. Eye-marker, Tachistoscope, Dual-projection, Out of focus, Aesthedes
12.30 h. Lunch
13.15 h. Functions and Requirements of a successful Brand Personality
14.00 h. Case
15.00 h. Tea
15.15 h. Judgement (your product?)
16.00 h. How to select an agency?
16.30 h. Discussion

THE C.P.C. FRAMEWORK

Both the C.P.C. field of experience and its broad scala of activities are

C.P.C. specializes in:
Product development
Concept evaluation
Product Performance
Corporate Identity (1)
Corporate Image
Name development (2)
Product Presentation
Brand Strategy
Brand Behaviour
Retail Formula (3)
Promotional Material

pictured here. It may serve you as a guide to what our organisation wants to be and what it achieved so far.
Amongst the specialized services you may find a concise, practice orientated diagram in the exhausting process of agency selection.
(part of the seminar too)

• Development Evaluation
• Performance
Company behind Product:
• Corporate Identity
• Product/Service Formula
• Presentation (packaging)
• Brand Behaviour
• Brandname-Development
• Promotional Material
• Rules of Conduct
• Retail Interior

nature / orientation	visualisation	communication
design	I aesthetical (grafical) design	II packaging design
product	III product presentation	IV brand (personality) development

YOUR OFFICE FOR ONE DAY

Claessens Product Consultants is located in Hilversum, Holland. In a green surrounding we have set up spacious offices, testing rooms, shop-simulation centres, studio's etc. All in order to be able to meet the high demands the trade asks for, all in order to safeguard the high sums companies have to invest when launching a new or

re-launching an existing product. It's an inspiring place, where artists, scientists and businessmen meet. It's your office for one day. Be our guest.

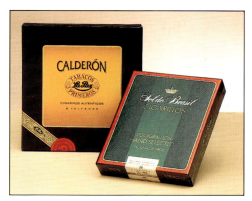

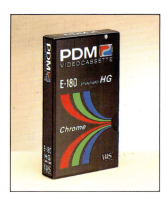

Claessens Product Consultants B.V.
the Brands and Personalities Company

Van Hengellaan 10 • 1217 AS Hilversum • Holland • Tel. 035 - 210551 • Fax. 035 - 217162 • Tlx. 43071

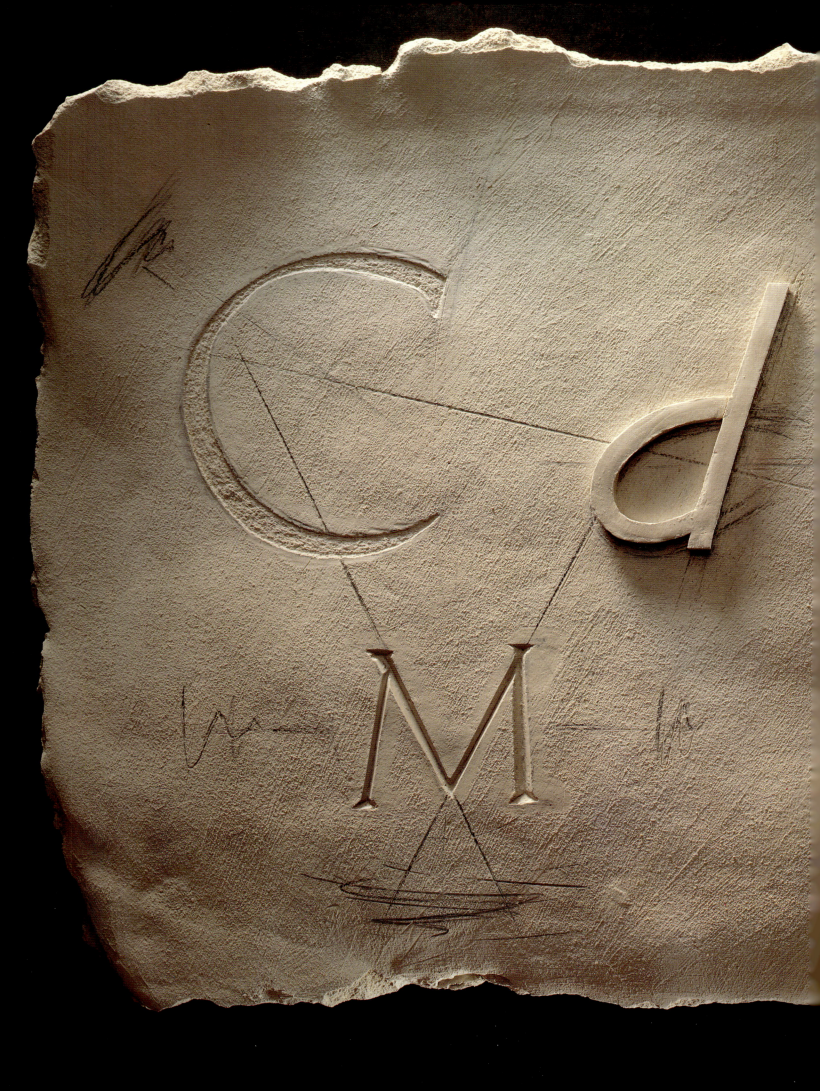

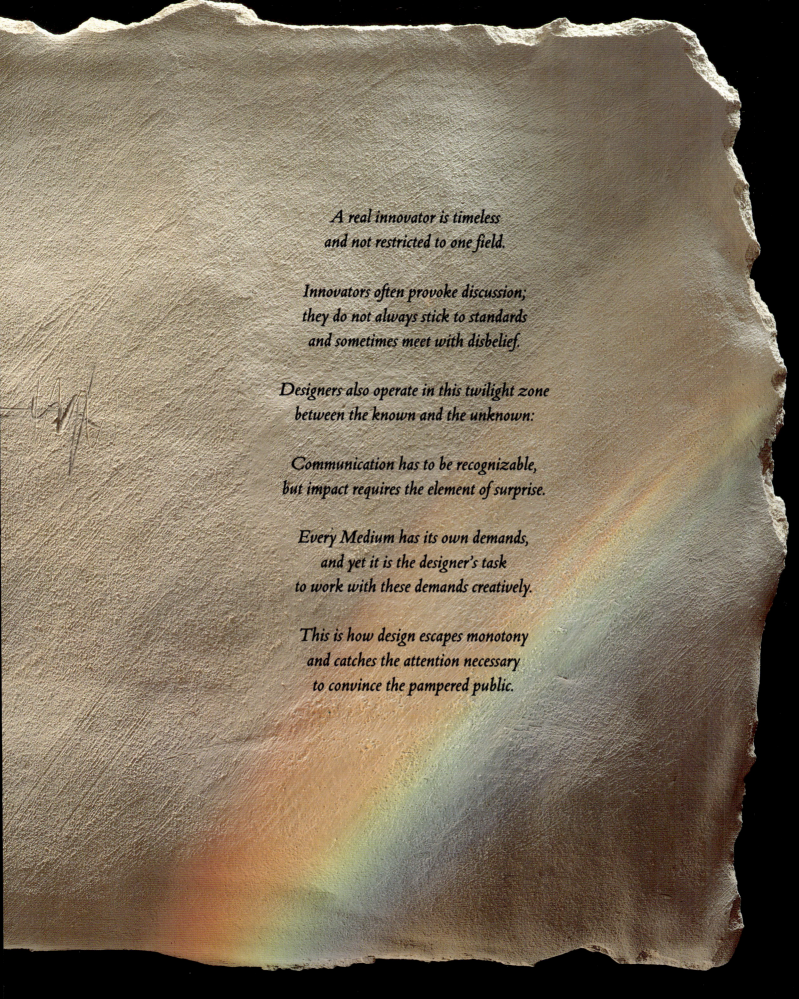

A real innovator is timeless
and not restricted to one field.

Innovators often provoke discussion;
they do not always stick to standards
and sometimes meet with disbelief.

Designers also operate in this twilight zone
between the known and the unknown:

Communication has to be recognizable,
but impact requires the element of surprise.

Every Medium has its own demands,
and yet it is the designer's task
to work with these demands creatively.

This is how design escapes monotony
and catches the attention necessary
to convince the pampered public.

VAN VELSEN *ontwerpburo* LAAPERSVELD 41 1213 VB HILVERSUM (035) 232705

"Our Daily Bread"

Varying from bare necessity to pure luxury and in a multitude of ap-

pearances. Always in motion, following trends in taste and aesthetics.

Millford-Van den Berg works hard at concept and design, lending their

clients a helping hand when it comes to packing products in a practical

and tasteful way. This is the daily work of more than twenty people,

who apply their feelings and their minds to create products that

please the eye, stimulate curiosity and make the mouth water.

That's our work. Your daily bread. And therefore ours, logically.

MILLFORD-VAN DEN BERG DESIGN B.V.
GROOT HAESEBROEKSEWEG 1, P.O. BOX 56, 2240 AB WASSENAAR
HOLLAND, TELEPHONE 01751-19100, TELEFAX 01751-13685

ARA/BDDP ★ Van den Bergh Foods ★ Biohorma ★ Boon ★ Campina Melkunie ★ Droste ★ General Biscuits ★ Grolsche Bierbrouwerij Nederland ★ Holland Canned Milk ★ Holland Casino's ★ Iglo ★ Zeepfabriek De Klok ★ Kortman-Intradal ★ Lever ★ Mora ★ Van Nelle ★ Network ★ Nutricia ★ Quaker Oats ★ Rikon Cosmetics ★ Royco ★ Schimmelpenninck ★ Schwarzkopf ★ TBRA ★ Vendex Food Group ★ Venz ★ Verbunt

NO STRATEGY,
NO SOLUTION.

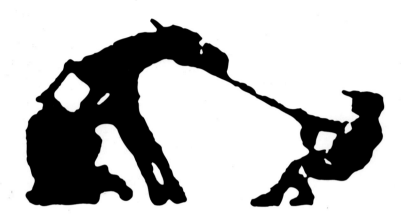

As a design studio, we're somewhat atypical.
We're not bowled over by an esthetic tour de force. Nor are we moved
to tears by the beauty of a logo. Or irresistibly driven to sing the praises
of the ultimate in styling. At least not in the first place.
Because at Stempels & Oster, we believe that design has to fit in.
With the product. With the company philosophy.
And most importantly, with the entire complex of advertising
communications. That's our initial concern. The fact that the product
developments, the corporate styles, the architectural designs and the
numerous other works of art that leave our studio also happen to
look good is something we tend to take for granted.
We consider it part of our own basic strategy.

Stempels & Oster

C O M M U N I C A T I V E   D E S I G N

DE KLENCKE 4, 1083 HH AMSTERDAM - BUITENVELDERT, TELEPHONE 020-46 42 46, FAX 66 12 921.

PACKAGING - CORPORATE IDENTITY - PRODUCT DEVELOPMENT - BELOW THE LINE - ARCHITECTURAL DESIGN AND STYLING FOR CANON, CC FRIESLAND, THE DUTCH DAIRY ASSOCIATION, THE DUTCH HEART SOCIETY, HOLLAND INVESTMENT GROUP,
ICI EUROPE, THE MINISTRY OF EDUCATION AND SCIENCE, ISEO MARKETING RESEARCH, LEIJTEN FOOTWEAR IMPORTS (TERRA PLANA, SIOUX), LEVER, NEDAN SWEETS, NESTLE, PLUKON, POSTBANK, PPGH/JWT, PTT TELECOM, QUAKER OATS,
R&C DIAMOND ACCESSORIES, VROOM & DREESMANN NEDERLAND, VRUMONA SOFT DRINKS (SOURCY, SISI, RIVELLA), ZIJ WOMEN'S WEAR AND OTHERS.

HARRY & ELISABETH ELBERS DESIGN

Vaartweg 36
NL-4731 RA Oudenbosch
Tel. 01652-16319
Fax: 01652-15204

Specialists in packaging and product design.

BOZELL DESIGN

BOZELL DESIGN B.V.

Bovenkerkerweg 2
NL-1185 XE Amstelveen
Tel. 020-47 69 76
Fax : 020-47 71 91

Ton Broek
Freek Claessens
Hans Erdmann
Peter Jacobs

Philip Kotler said recently : "It is no longer enough to satisfy the customer. You have to delight him." From this point of view the Bozell Design team wants to work side by side with clients on solutions which your target group can identify with.

Whether this involves shelf domination by means of package design or optimalizing the accessibility of shops, shopping centres, health centres or offices. Bozell Design is "close to the customer".
Both ours as well as yours.

BOZELL DESIGN

BOZELL DESIGN B.V.

Bovenkerkerweg 2
NL-1185 XE Amstelveen
Tel.   020-47 69 76
Fax : 020-47 71 91

Ton Broek
Freek Claessens
Hans Erdmann
Peter Jacobs

Philip Kotler said recently : "It is no longer enough to satisfy the customer. You have to delight him." From this point of view the Bozell Design team wants to work side by side with clients on solutions which your target group can identify with.

Whether this involves shelf domination by means of package design or optimalizing the accessibility of shops, shopping centres, health centres or offices. Bozell Design is "close to the customer".
Both ours as well as yours.

ANN MAES INDUSTRIAL DESIGN

Terlostraat 3
NL-5571 KW Bergeyk
Tel. 04975-4455
Fax : 04975-4555

Product design, development
and promotion.

Editorial activities and PR.
Correspondent for Abitare,
Villas, Signs & Structures, a.o.

Design Label 1980 /
Design Centre Brussels.
Intercom Award 1984 –
1st lighting prize / Int.
Biennal Interieur Kortrijk.
Design Label 1987 / IoN.

Products included in
the design collection
of several museums of
modern art.

ANN MAES INDUSTRIAL DESIGN

Terlostraat 3
NL-5571 KW Bergeyk
Tel. 04975-4455
Fax: 04975-4555

Product design, development and promotion.

Editorial activities and PR. Correspondent for Abitare, Villas, Signs & Structures, a.o.

Design Label 1980 / Design Centre Brussels. Intercom Award 1984 – 1st lighting prize / Int. Biennal Interieur Kortrijk. Design Label 1987 / IoN.

Products included in the design collection of several museums of modern art.

THE CREATIVE CREDO

Continuously in search for creative solutions. That's our credo and our USP at the same time. Let's introduce ourselves: a multi-disciplined graphic design unit which is capable of producing a variety of items:

- advertising concepts and development
- corporate identity styling/trademarks
- magazines/journals
- product- and corporate brochures
- annual reports
- direct mailing development & production

Our creative attention to detail and the traditional craftsmanship is combined with highly advanced tools like computer aided design systems.

A different aproach for each discipline and a fanatical concern for quality: the guarantee of a succesful result.

KOPERDRAAD DESIGN/REKLAME,
Noordereinde 13, P.O. Box 145, 1243 ZJ 's Graveland, The Netherlands
Telephone (31) (0) 35 - 63435 Telefax (31) (0) 35 - 63258

Designers

France
France
Frankreich

DESGRIPPES & ASSOCIATES

International Agency for Communication by Design

18 bis, avenue de la Motte Picquet
75007 Paris - France
Tél. : (1) 45 50 34 45
Fax : (1) 45 51 96 60

THE CREATIVE PASSION

DESGRIPPES & ASS.

AGENCE INTERNATIONALE
DE COMMUNICATION
PAR LE DESIGN

*BRAND IDENTITY
AND PACKAGING: RoC.*

*BOTTLE DESIGN/
FRAGRANCE:
BOUCHERON.*

*CORPORATE IDENTITY:
CRÉDIT AGRICOLE.*

*IMAGE-ORIENTED
PRODUCTS: PECHINEY.*

*PACKAGING:
CANDEREL RANGE.*

*PRODUCT DESIGN:
GUY DEGRENNE.*

*RETAIL ENVIRONMENT:
SONIA RYKIEL.*

LE CLAN DESIGN

61, rue Servan
75011 PARIS
Tél. : (1) 48.05.82.82
Fax 48.05.82.09

Dominique BELLE
Création

Jean-Jacques URVOY
Marketing

Strenghened by their own experiences within the pioneer French agencies of the 70's Dominique BELLE and Jean-Jacques URVOY have created and launched new working systems which unable them to lead their projects rightly and safely to a successful conclusion.

Thus, the CLAN DESIGN is becoming a new reference in the world of design of the 90's, a new school of design.

AU CŒUR DU CLAN, LE TALENT

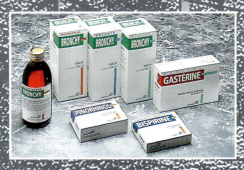  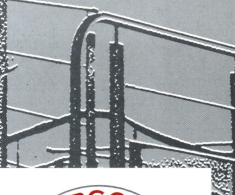

lacombe
pingaud

P A C K A G I N G

Xavier Lacombe, creative director,
and Christophe Pingaud, marketing director,
became partners in 1987
and started the Lacombe-Pingaud Design Group.

OUR TRADE : CREATION

Creation is specifically our business, in every different aspect of design.

Design always expresses the identity and environment of a company or a product. We never propose an image which is not backed by a strategy, nor a strategy which is not converted into an image. We think that this strategic background has to lead the graphic expression to an ideal blending of style, relevance, impact and peculiarity.

OUR TEAM : FLEXIBLE AND INTERNATIONAL

We believe in an efficient structure which is light and flexible, as comprehensive in its skills as it is sharp in its own creative requirements.

As the market for consumer goods and therefore design itself has spread world-wide, we are convinced that the best reply is to put the experiences and sensibilities of young Latin and Anglo-Saxon designers together.

We have built up an accomplished team of full-time and free-lace talents of all skills: design, art direction, desktop publishing, artwork, illustration, copywriting.

OUR ACTIVITIES : ALL FACETS OF DESIGN

From the same basic creative philosophy, we can either create, revive, adapt or even harmonize all the different communication media of any company. We can thus produce corporate identity, brand typography, packaging, house magazines, press packs, corporate brochures, annual reports...

OUR CLIENTS : FROM SMALLER
COMPANIES TO INTERNATIONAL GROUPS

Thanks to our creative resources and flexibility, we are able to fulfil the requirements of the marketing manager in a large multinational group as efficiently as the needs of the managing director in a national company.

IDENTITE VISUELLE

EDITION

7, rue Robert Fleury
75015 Paris
Tél. : (1) 45.67.01.04
Fax : (1) 45.67.81.37

CONTACT :
Xavier Lacombe
Christophe Pingaud

OVA'O

24, rue Feydeau
75002 Paris
Tél. : 40.28.00.92
Fax : 40.28.00.93
Date de création : juin 1988

OVA'O
L'IMAGE DE MARQUE

L'IMAGE DE MARQUE PERMET DE TRANSMETTRE
LES VALEURS ET LA CULTURE DE L'ENTREPRISE,
D'IDENTIFIER SES PRODUITS ET SES SERVICES.

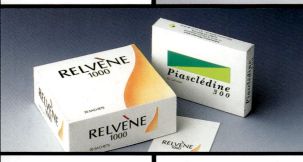

DANS LA BATAILLE DE LA COMMUNICATION,
L'IMAGE DE MARQUE EST L'ÉTENDARD
DE L'ENTREPRISE À LA CONQUÊTE DE SES MARCHÉS,
SON IDENTITÉ.

DISTINCTIV DESIGN
A R D A I N

DISTINCTIV DESIGN - Jean-Pierre Ardain S.A.
17, rue du Pont-aux-Choux - 75003 PARIS
Tél. : (1) 48 04 77 70
Fax : (1) 48 04 39 26
Contact client :
Jean-Pierre Ardain, Patrick Domingie

97

Created in 1973,
Carré Noir was the first to introduce
a marketing approach
to the graphic design field.
Through the multi-disciplined approach
of Carré Noir's nine separate
- but integrated - divisions,
Carré Noir can respond to the total spectrum
of a company's design challenges.

Corporate Identity
■
Packaging
■
Product Design
■
Environmental Design
■
Point of Purchase Design
■
Industrial Design
■
Public Relations
■
Licensing
■
Merchandising

EUROPE
Carré Noir S.A.
82-84, boulevard des Batignolles
75850 Paris Cedex 17. France
Tél. (1) 42 94 02 27. Fax (1) 42 94 06 78
Télex 281 237 F

■

NORTH AMERICA
Carré Noir Inc New York
Morris Zand
244 Fifth Avenue - NY 10001. USA
Tel. (212) 645 0191. Fax (212) 645 1086

■

ASIA
Agence Carré Noir Tokyo
Akasaka Q Building 5 F
7.9.5 Akasaka Minato-ku. Tokyo 107. Japan
Tel (03) 582 1201. Fax (03) 582 1202

MEMBRE
ASSOCIATION DESIGN COMMUNICATION

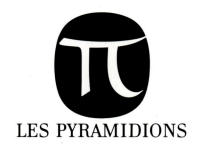

LES PYRAMIDIONS

AMIENS

GRÈS

PARIS

SAITAMA BANK

CĒRABATI

L'ALSACIENNE

ERATO

P.RÉFÉRENCE
BUREAU DE CRÉATION

Un packaging est une association de formes, de signes graphiques, de visuels, de couleurs... construisant l'image d'un produit. Le packaging est le principal élément porteur de l'identité visuelle de ce produit. De plus en plus d'opérations et de matériels sont créés autour du produit pour mieux le faire connaître et mieux le faire vendre. Afin d'optimiser ce double objectif, la cohérence entre l'identité visuelle du produit et celle du matériel créé est indispensable.
P.RÉFÉRENCE, Agence de Design, crée et rénove des packagings et se fait une priorité d'assurer l'homogénéité de tout le matériel qui va graviter autour du produit. Aucun élément porteur de la marque ne doit être négligé : argumentaires, leaflets, notices, fiches techniques, PLV, offres promotionnelles... doivent impérativement s'inscrire au sein d'une charte graphique cohérente avec l'identité visuelle du produit. Ainsi, nous contribuons à affirmer et à conforter l'image de vos marques sur le marché.

*P*ackaging is a combination of forms, graphic symbols and colors... portraying a product's image. The packaging is the principal element carrying the product's visual identity.
More and more, promotions and support material are created around the product for better recognition and therefore, increased sales. In order to achieve this, the coherence between the product's visual identity and its promotional material is essential.
P.RÉFÉRENCE, Agence de Design, creates as well as updates the packaging design of product lines with priority given to the uniformity of all elements carrying the brand name and logotype: sell sheets, leaflets, point of purchase materials and promotional offers must all be incorporated into the graphic image of the product line.

P.RÉFÉRENCE (1) 42.89.11.48
16, RUE VÉZELAY 75008 PARIS
FAX (1) 45.61.92.79
CONTACT : FABRICE PELTIER

1 - CHOLLET S.A.
Création packaging d'une gamme de produits d'entretien pour voiture, METALFORM.
CHOLLET S.A.
Package design for METALFORM, automotive product line.

2 - DIPARCO
Rénovation packaging de la gamme des après-rasages H POUR HOMME.
DIPARCO
Packaging redesign for H POUR HOMME after shave line.

3 - SYSTÈME U
Création packaging pour steak haché SYSTÈME U
SYSTÈME U
Package design for SYSTÈME U chopped steak.

4 - BENCKISER ST-MARC
Création packaging de produits de soins pour cuirs, BARANNE MEUBLES ET VÊTEMENTS.
BENCKISER ST-MARC
Package design for BARANNE, cream products for leather furniture and clothing.

5 - DIPARCO
Rénovation packaging de la gamme maquillage teint GEMEY.
DIPARCO
Package redesign of the GEMEY fluid make-up line.

6/7 - BENCKISER ST-MARC
Rénovation packaging de deux produits d'entretien pour la maison, SAINT-MARC MÉNAGE et SAINT-MARC CRÈME.
BENCKISER ST-MARC
Package design for SAINT-MARC MÉNAGE and SAINT-MARC CRÈME, cleaning product for the home.

8 - BENCKISER ST-MARC
Création packaging d'une graisse pour cuir, BARANNE GRAISSE.
BENCKISER ST-MARC
Package design for a new product in the BARANNE product line, "BARANNE GRAISSE", for the care of leather shoes.

9 - L'ORÉAL
Création packaging d'un nouveau produit de soin haute performance, ELSÈVE CONCENTRÉ SPÉCIAL POINTES.
L'ORÉAL
Package design for CONCENTRÉ SPÉCIAL POINTES, a new high performance product in the ELSÈVE product line.

1

2

3

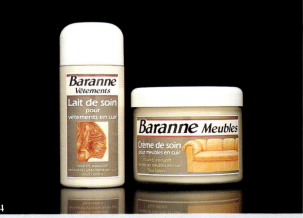

4

5

6

7

8

9

CRABTREE HALL   PLAN CREATIF

70 Crabtree Lane
London SW6 6LT
tél. (071) 381 8755
fax.(071) 385 9575

10, rue Mercœur
F-75011 Paris
tél. 1 43 70 60 60
fax.1 43 70 96 29

Contacts :
Gérard LECŒUR
Linda SHOPPEE

Contacts :
Claude BRAUNSTEIN
Clément ROUSSEAU

From product design to corporate
identity, from packaging to exhibition
stands, from sales points to catalogs,
Crabtree Hall / Plan Créatif knows
how to meet corporate needs.

Du design de produit à l'image de
marque, du packaging aux stands,
des lieux de vente aux catalogues,
Crabtree Hall / Plan Créatif sait faire
tout ce que dit et représente
l'entreprise.

CRABTREE HALL
PLAN CREATIF

P R O D U I T

Conception

de produits nouveaux,

amélioration

de produits existants,

étude de panneaux

de contrôle et synoptiques,

étude de coloration,

système de transports.

DOMENA fer à repasser

PORCHER gamme de robinetterie Porphyre

RATP métro Boa

C O M M U N I C A T I O N

Identité visuelle,

signalétique,

édition,

packaging,

image de marque.

TECHNAL catalogue produits

LA PROCURE identité visuelle
CLEVELAND BUSINESS CENTRE identité visuelle

OCTAGON CENTRE centre commercial
PACO SWEATERS magasins franchisés

LONDIS identité visuelle, packaging

E N V I R O N N E M E N T

Expositions,

stands,

aménagement

de points de vente,

muséographie.

CONOCO stations service JET

CRABTREE HALL
PLAN CREATIF

Brand Identity
Ambition

HOTEL
Duc de Saint-Simon
PARIS

THIS MAGIC PLACE
IN THE HEART OF PARIS
DESERVED A GRAND IMAGE.

What does a small, refined, and ambitious hotel, frequented by Lauren Bacall and Françoise Sagan, do in order to become a prominent Parisian and international reference? It calls on the services of brand identity specialists, professionnals who combine strategic vision and visual inspiration in order to create a brand identity that tells a story and evokes an era. Professionnals that make the identity come alive through a book and other materials that illustrate the charm and the elegance of the hotel. Finally, a team that assists its clients in the concrete realization of their proposed solutions. Creativity, strategy and technique for success stories.

STYLE MARQUE
AGENCE CONSEIL EN IMAGE DE MARQUE

PARIS

10 RUE DES MOULINS 75001 PARIS - TÉL : 42 96 16 78 - CONTACT : YVES RONIN

PGJ

1, RUE D'ARGENSON
75008 PARIS
TÉL. : 42.68.08.45
FAX : 42.68.01.21

RÉFÉRENCES

AIR FRANCE
BESNIER
B.N.
BONGRAIN
BRIDEL
B.S.N.
CIBA GEIGY
DEGRENNE
DELACRE
DIEPAL
DUCROS
ENTREMONT
FLODOR
HUMAN - PHARM
LARDENOIS
LINDT
POMONA
SAINT MICHEL
SEITA
VIVAGEL...

ESPACE
INTUITION
5, rue des Hospitalières Saint Gervais - 75004 Paris
Tél. : (1) 42.71.08.12 - Fax : (1) 42.71.13.72

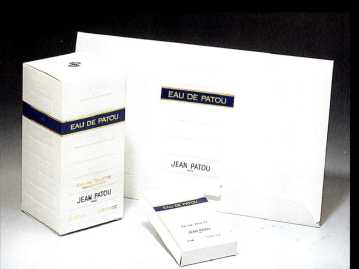

DESIGN STRATEGY S.A.

Villa Souchet
105, avenue Gambetta - 75020 Paris
Tél.: (1) 43.66.55.33 - Télex: 213620
Fax: (1) 43.66.79.00
Established in 1982

Philippe RASQUINET
Chairman:
Design Strategy
Co-Chairman: MTDS

Jim WATERS
General Manager/
Creative Manager:
Design Strategy
Managing Partner: MTDS

PERMANENT STAFF

Number of staff: 140   (France) 65

SPECIALISED DEPARTMENTS, SUBSIDIARIES

MARKETING IMAGE: 105, Villa Souchet
avenue Gambetta - F 75020 Paris
Tél.: 43.66.55.33.
General Manager: Jean-Louis DUCLOS
Image Evaluation and strategy
ORCHESTRA: Tour Gallieni 2
36, avenue Gallieni - F93160 Bagnolet
Tél.: (1) 43.60.49.25
General Manager: Claude MEILLET
Artistic Manager: David HAWKINS
Communications strategies and systems
MINALE TATTERSFIELD:
The Courtyard
37 Sheen Road - Richmond Surrey GB
TW 91 A J - Tél.: (81) 948.79.79
Managing Partners:
Marcello MINALE
Brian TATTERSFIELD
Identity, Product and Industrial Design, Packaging, Print

Representative offices in: Brussels, London, New York, Milan, Madrid, Cologne, Casablanca, Hong Kong, Osaka, Brisbane, Sydney.

Trade Federation: ADC
Awards won: Packaging Oscar 1987-88. Logo Award for Bull.

For further information contact: Philippe Rasquinet, Elisabeth Assor.

PHILOSOPHY AND POSITIONNING

Design Strategy is a consultancy specialised in Corporate Image, in the creation and implementation of visual identities in the permanent media.
Our vocation is to help companies to discover the strengths of their personalities, to define their image strategy and to implement it by creating a strong coherent and durable identity. Fundamentally, Design Strategy considers that design is a strategic management tool.
To-day our clients require us to have expertise and experience which are truly international.
We have merged with one of the leading British design consultancies - Minale, Tattersfield. Together we have offices in 13 European countries and also in Africa, in Japan and in the United States.
According to the *Financial Times* classification we are number seven in the worldwide design consultancy table. Our ambition is to help French and European companies to export more and to be more competitive in their markets by practising a better design policy.

SPECIALISED SERVICES

- Visual Identity
  - evaluation and image strategy
  - creation of visual identities
  - implementation and identity manuals
- Environmental Design
  - analysis and strategy
  - creation and concepts
  - organisation and distribution systems
  - architecture
- Packaging
  - evaluation, marketing strategy
  - graphic creation

- conditioning creation
- brand creation
- Product design
  - value analysis
  - style
  - conditioning creation
  - brand creation

EQUIPMENT AND METHODS

Design Strategy's approach is global, rational and creative; it consists of successive stages:

Analysis and visual audit: evaluation of the personality of the company, of its competitive positioning and its communication in the form of research, internal and external interviews and an audit of its activity sector.

Creative research: depending on the positioning and image strategy adopted, numerous ideas are explored before a final identity choice is made.

Internal communication: meetings and documents explain the new system.

Implementation: the new identity is applied to all the company's visual manifestations.

External communication: launching of the new identity. Creation and publication of the identity manual.

HOLDING COMPANY

Minale Tattersfield - Design Strategy Group

MAIN SHAREHOLDERS

Philippe Rasquinet, Jim Waters

MANAGERS AND MAIN STAFF

Philippe Rasquinet (Chairman), Jim Waters (Creative Manager), Mike McNeilage (Manager of the Product and Packaging Design Division)

TURNOVER

MTDS Group 1989   104 Million French Francs

GROSS MARGIN

1989 France   35 Million French Francs

CLIENTS

Corporate Identity
- B.N.P.
- Bull
- Calvados
- Caisse d'Epargne Ecureuil
- Crédit du Maroc
- G.M.F.
- Giat Industries
- Harrods
- H.L.M.
- Matra
- Ocean Oil
- Rhône-Poulenc
- S.N.C.F.
- SUEZ
- Trésor public
- U.A.P.
- Union de Banques à Paris

Environmental Design
- London Airport - Heathrow
- Aubépain
- Banque Marocaine du Commerce Extérieur
- Climat de France
- France Telecom
- S.N.C.F.

Packaging
- B.P.
- Findus
- Martini
- Charal
- Schweppes
- Waterman
- Johnnie Walker

DESIGN STRATEGY S.A.

Villa Souchet,
105, avenue Gambetta - 75020 Paris
Tél. : 43.66.55.33 - Télex : 213620
Télécopie : 43.66.79.00
Date de création : 1982

Une liaison durable tient souvent à de petites choses

Conseil permanent en identité pour les plus grandes entreprises européennes

VITRAC DESIGN

PARIS-MADRID-TOKYO

60, rue d'Avron 75020 PARIS
Tél.: (1) 40-24-08-00 *Fax: (1) 40-24-08-12*

VITRAC
DESIGN PROSPECTIF

"Créer pour nourrir les stratégies des entreprises."

Les concepts, Les produits.   Les produits, Les corporates.   Les Packagings.

ARCHITRAL

28, rue Broca
75005 Paris France
Tél. : 33 (1) 45.35.04.04
Fax : 33 (1) 43.36.38.98
Télex : 205 616

Marketing - Merchandising -
Interior architecture - Shopping centers -
Product design - Industrial design.

Alcan, Aluminium industry - ASF, French freeways -
Darty, House electricals - Fnac, Culture and leisure - Fnac Musique, Records -
Galeries Lafayette, Department store -
Grand Optical, Lens - Merlin Gerin, Electro mecanics -
Photo Hall, Photo shops - Photo Service, Photo shops -
R.A.T.P., French metropolitain -
SARI, Shopping centers developer -
SEGECE, Shopping centers developer - SONY.

Contact : Gérard Barrau.

Architral Agency

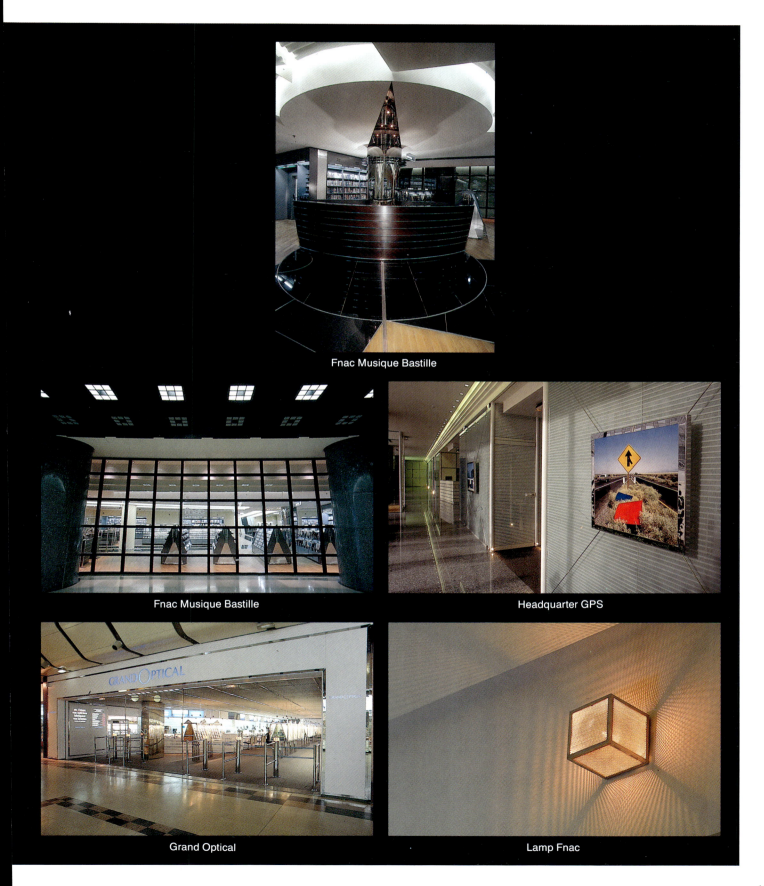

Fnac Musique Bastille

Fnac Musique Bastille

Headquarter GPS

Grand Optical

Lamp Fnac

Designers

Germany

Allemagne

Deutschland

WINDI V

DES

EIMSBÜTTELER CHAUSSEE 23   2000 HAMB

DERLICH Ⓦ

NCY

TEL 040-431708-0   FAX 040-4300586

OLAF GAUMER

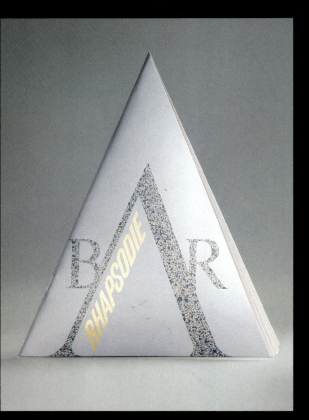

Holzhausenstraße 22   D 6000 Frankfurt am Main 1

Neue Anschrift ab 1. 1. 1991: Schumannstraße 10

OLAF GAUMER

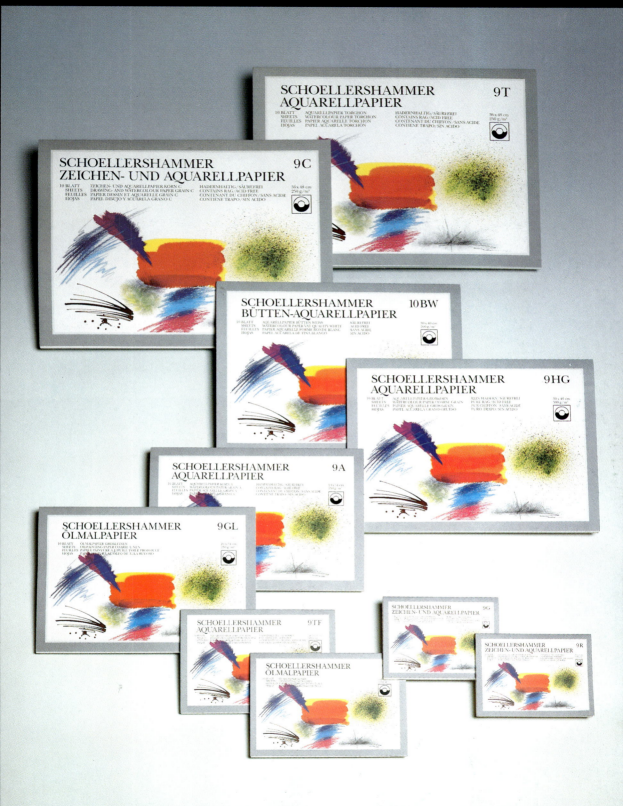

Telefon 0 69/55 04 15   55 04 16   55 04 17   59 08 68   Telefax 0 69/5 96 23 53

Neue Telefon- und Fax-Nummern ab 1. 1. 1991

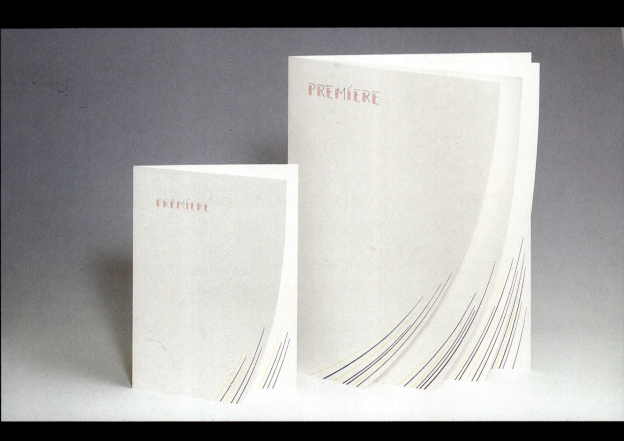

Holzhausenstraße 22   D 6000 Frankfurt am Main 1
Neue Anschrift ab 1. 1. 1991: Schumannstraße 10

OLAF GAUMER

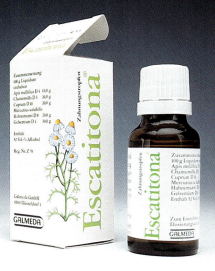

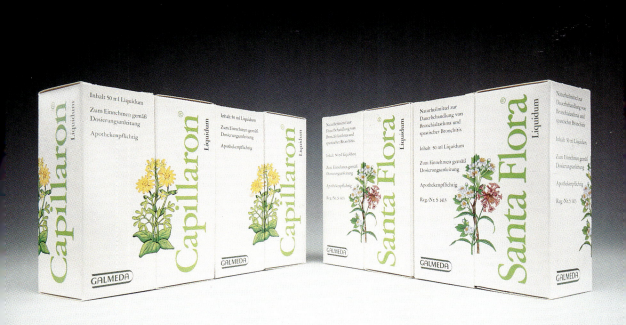

OLAF GAUMER

Holzhausenstraße 22   D 6000 Frankfurt am Main 1
Neue Anschrift ab 1. 1. 1991: Schumannstraße 10

OLAF GAUMER

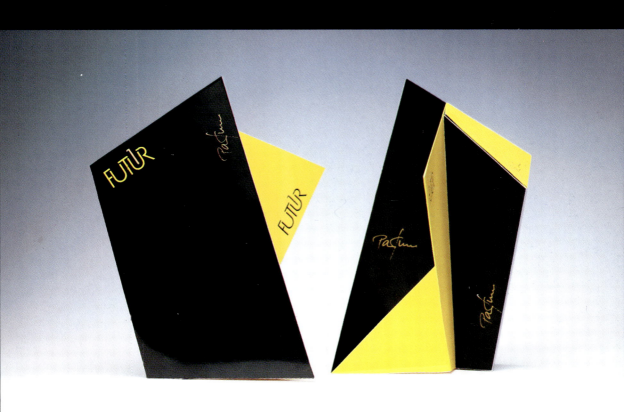

Telefon 0 69/55 04 15   55 04 16   55 04 17   59 08 68   Telefax 0 69/5 96 23 53
Neue Telefon- und Fax-Nummern ab 1. 1. 1991

Designers

Switzerland

Suisse

Schweiz

S+INTERPUBLIC SA

ADVERTISING AND PUBLIC RELATIONS

Via Pradello
CH-6934 Lugano-Bioggio
Tel.   091-59 18 61
Fax : 091-59 20 60

We plan national and international campaigns. We design advertising and information media in all dimensions, we form appearances. We visualize messages in illustrations, photographs, films and videos. We produce text, typesetting, reproductions and printing in a variety of techniques. We build models in all sizes, 3-dimensional advertising media and exhibition stands.

We work for the success of our clients.

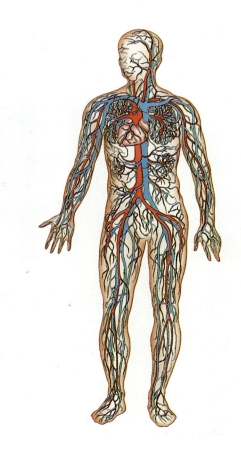

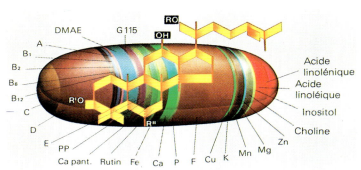

DMAE · G 115 · RO · OH
A
B₁
B₂
B₆
B₁₂
C · R'O
D · R''
E
PP
Ca pant. · Rutin · Fe · Ca · P · F · Cu · K · Mn · Mg · Zn
Acide linolénique
Acide linoléique
Inositol
Choline

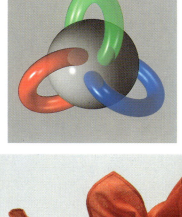

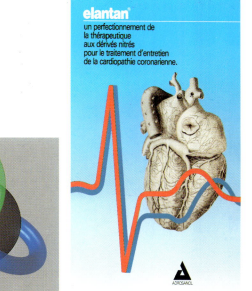

elantan®
un perfectionnement de
la thérapeutique
aux dérivés nitrés
pour le traitement d'entretien
de la cardiopathie coronarienne.

ADROSANOL

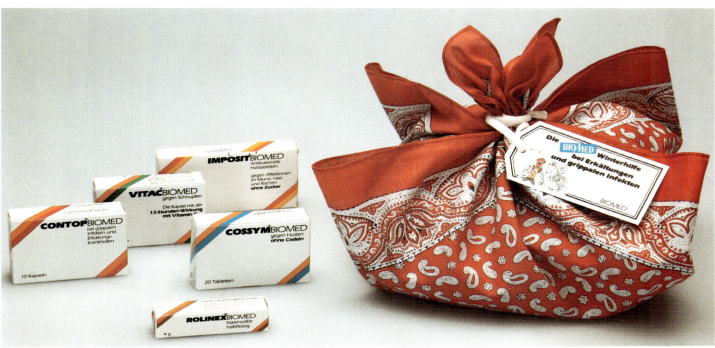

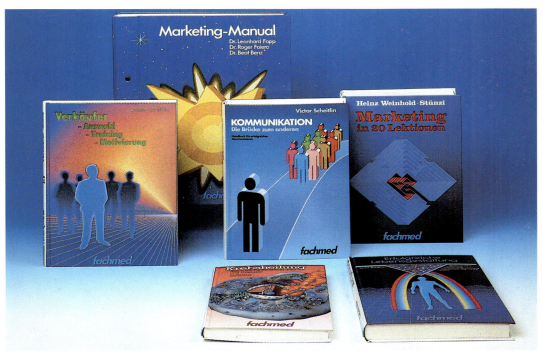

Designers

Italy
Italie
Italien

PAOLO BRAGGION

Via Giuseppe Verdi, 20
I-35010 Limena (Padova)
Tel. 049-76 73 57

Agents:
LUCATELLO S.p.A.
Via G. D'Annunzio, 75
I-31030 Biancade (Treviso)
Tel. 0422-84 91 01
Fax: 0422-84 99 99
Telex: 410595

MOBILEGNO FATTORI S.r.l.
Industria Mobili Componibili
Via Postumia Est
I-31042 Fagarè (Treviso)
Tel. 0422-79 00 16
79 02 84
Fax: 0422-79 04 72

Born in Padua, architect, lives and works in Padua and Milan. Has been visiting professor at the Institute of design in Fribourg. Exhibits in Italy and abroad. In 1984, held conferences about design for the French Ministry of Art. His works are shown at the MOMA in N.Y. Has a didactic activity abroad.

ARDUINI & SALVEMINI

Via Ciro Menotti, 33
I-20129 Milano
Tel. 02-22 26 51
         294 099 94

Since 1976, Gianni Arduini and Gianfranco Salvemini have concentrated on industrial design, with main emphasis on consumer durables. Their interest lies in applying new materials and techniques.
Winner of the 1984 "Compasso d'Oro".

Gianni Arduini e Gianfranco Salvemini si occupano di industrial design dal 1976 progettando prevalentemente beni durevoli con interesse all'impiego di materiali e tecniche nuove.
Vincitori "Compasso d'Oro", 1984.

Seit 1976, Gianni Arduini und Gianfranco Salvemini beschäftigen sich mit Industrie-Design. Sie entwerfen hauptsächlich Gebrauchsgüter und interessieren sich für die Anwendung neuer Materialien und Techniken.
Sieger des "Compasso d'Oro", 1984.

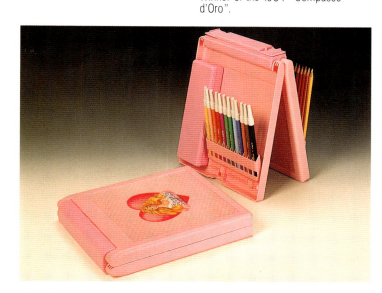

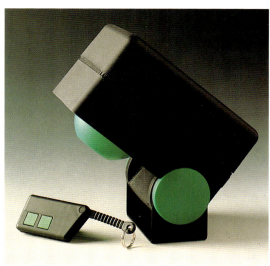

Designers

Portugal
Portugal
Portugal

JORGE CARVALHO & LEONOR PERRY, LDA.

Rua Morais Soares, 7-1.º Dto.
P-1900 Lisboa
Tel. 351 - 1 82 05 44
          83 38 87
Fax: 351-1-82 55 81

Illustrations, animatics for cinema,
layout, final arts, storyboards,
mock ups, stands, printing, silk,
scren and offset.

Find out what we have to offer.
Fax: 351-1-82 55 81.

Ilustrações, animação para cinema,
maquetas, artes finais, storyboards,
mock, ups, stands, impresso
em serigrafia e offset.

Descubra o que temos para lhe
oferecer.
Fax: 351-1-82 55 81

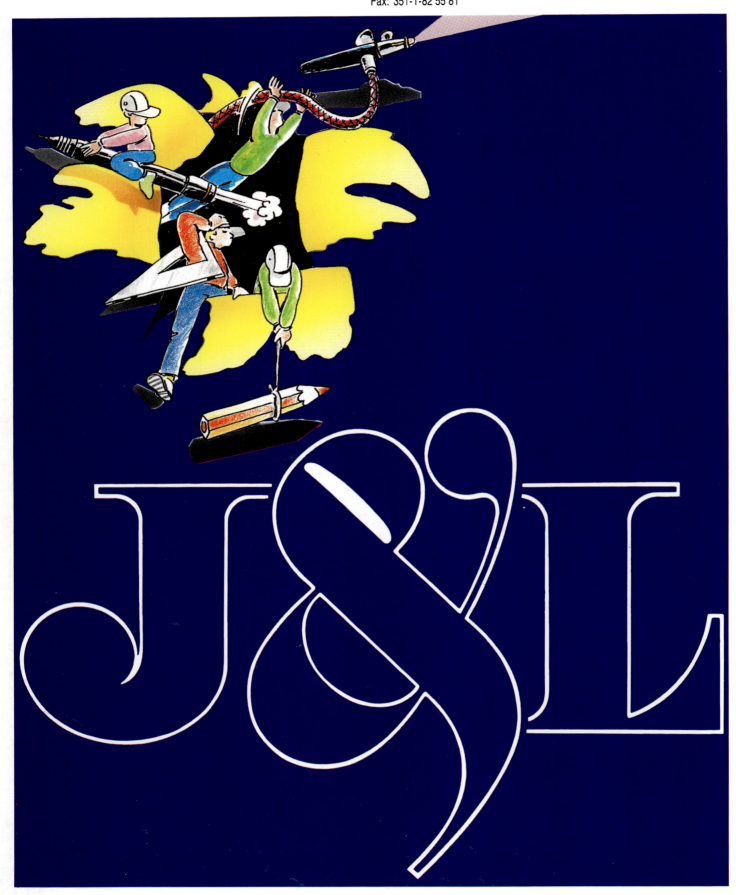

SERISE EXPRESSO

Praceta Pintor José Félix
Lote 83 Loja Esq.
Reboleira Sul - 2700 AMADORA
Telefs. 0351 - 1 - 97 51 95
Fax. 0351 - 1 - 97 32 09
97 51 95

Impressão, offset e serigrafia:

Revistas, brochuras, cartazes,
catálogos, linhas gráficas,
autocolantes, T-shirts

Descubra o que temos para lhe
oferecer
Fax 351 1 97 32 09
351 1 97 51 95

Printing, silk screen and offset:

Magazines, posters, catalogues,
T-shirts, brochure

To find out whay we have to offer

HENRIQUE NOGUEIRA

Rua Alfredo Cunha, 217-1.º
Salas 5/6
P-4450 Matosinhos
Tel. 93 47 25
Fax: 93 86 40
Telex: 25211

Illustration.
Graphic design.
Airbrush work.
Computer Design.

Ilustração.
Design gráfico.
Técnica em aérografo.
Design computorizado.

Illustration.
Graphisme.
Technique en aérographe.
Images de synthèse.

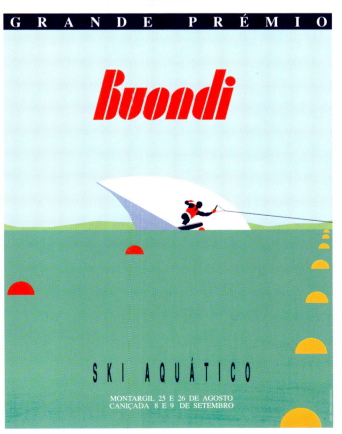

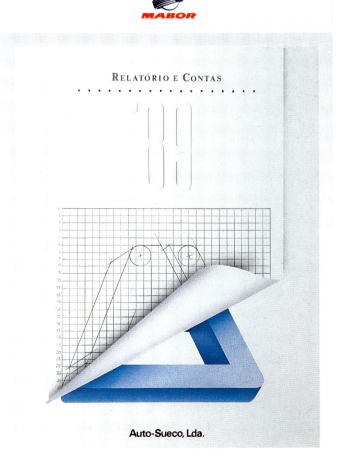

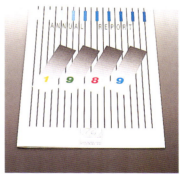

DESIGN & PUBLICIDADE

RUA CÂNDIDO DE FIGUEIREDO, 78, 2.º-DTO.
1500 LISBOA PORTUGAL
TELEFS. 78 82 81 - 74 19 46
TELEFAX: 78 40 36

FILIPE COSTA, DESIGNER

Seat : Av. do Uruguai, 34-7.º C
P-1500 Lisboa
Tel. 714 38 26
Atelier : Complexo do Paço
Paço do Lumiar
P-1600 Lisboa
Tel. 758 73 51
Fax : 759 83 42
Telex : 60297

Corporate image, graphic design, pictography, brochures, packaging and interior design for exhibitions. Full service design studio.

– PORTOBELO – Vilamoura, Timeshare multimedia advertising campaign.
– UDEX, Corporate image for importing company.
– GASIN, Medical Conference on Oxygen therapy.

– Corporate image for : ITACO, Fixing modular systems ; HOMOGEST, Human resources ; L&D ; Livestock center for pig breeding.
– ALFA LISBOA HOTEL, Graphic image for hotel services.

141

QUATRO PONTO QUATRO

**GABINETE TÉCNICO
DE DESIGN INDUSTRIAL, LDA.**

Rua José Magro, Lote 4 Traseiras
1300 LISBOA
Telef. 64 82 30 - 64 82 39
Telex 61606 QUAQUA P
Fax 64 90 80

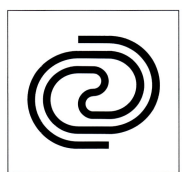

PUBLISTILO

Transportes Integrados de Mercadorias,lda.

ERMI

DAVID DE CARVALHO
TRAV. CONDE DA RIBEIRA 21 - 1.º ESQ. 1300 LISBOA
TELEFONE : 362 08 63

Designers

Spain
Espagne
Spanien

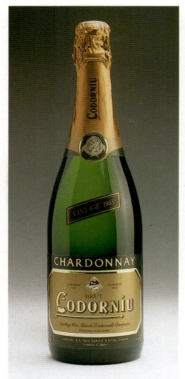

Laboratorio Ribas Morales

ARIBAU, 324 ENTLO. C
08006 BARCELONA - ESPAÑA
TEL. (93) 200 49 85 - FAX (93) 200 49 85

IRF, SA COMUNICACION Y RELACIONES PUBLICAS

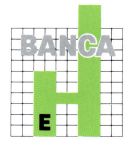

EL DISEÑO DE LA LUZ

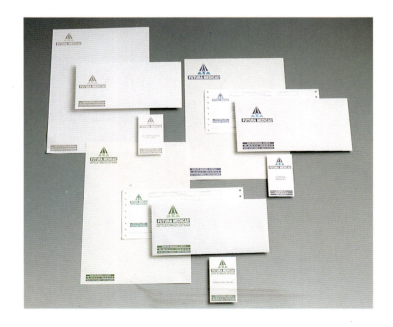

T+N ASOCIADOS
TORRES NAVARRO

C/. Isabel la Católica, 19, 6.º
Tel. (96) 352 07 18
Télex 63165
Fax 6-352 86 51
46004 VALENCIA (Spain)

GABINETE ESPECIALIZADO EN LA IMAGEN INTEGRAL DE EMPRESA

Nuestro objetivo es proporcionar a nuestros
clientes el asesoramiento y la creación de la imagen
global de su empresa. Aumentar por la imagen sus ventas
y darle un posicionamiento a nivel comunicativo visual imprescindible
en el mundo comercial actual.
Numerosas empresas de España, Japón, EE.UU., nos han confiado sus servicios.

FMBV
THE CORPORATION FOR COSMETIC DENTISTRY

C.B. L'Eliana

HiPODROMO

SPANISHIKI

AERO DENTAL '90

CRISPIEL LIMPIEZA

CLASSIC CAR

UAV
Lacados y Anodizados de Valencia, S.A.

edisersa
Edificaciones Ferrando s.a.

punto y aparte

Josep Pujol i Perdigó

Ganduxer 16, ático 1ª
Tel: (93) 209 14 94 - Fax: (93) 209 37 49
E-08021 BARCELONA

Diseño gráfico. Imagen corporativa. Packaging. Monografías y folletos para la industria farmacéutica, veterinaria y cosmética.

TAURO

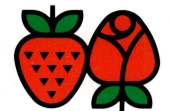

ROSSYL ESENCIAS

CODASTE NAVIERA DE RECREO

GIMNASIO PEDRALBES

GRAN CASINO LAS PALMAS

PROMOCION TURISTICA

VINOS DE CATALUÑA

MATERNOVA MODA PRE-MAMA

VIBA IMPORT - EXPORT

LIMPIEZA DOMESTICA

FAUX-CHON ROTISSERIE - IBIZA

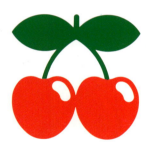

PACHA DISCOTECA

NIDO INDUSTRIAL

CASTILLA SERVICIOS DE MENSAJERIA

MOBILIARIO

VAGAMA IMPRESORES

LABORATORIOS VITA

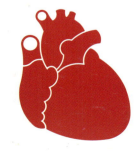

PARKE-DAVIS SIMBOLO PARA PRODUCTO

SISTEMAS DE ARCHIVO

FAST FOOD

Josep Pujol i Perdigó

Ganduxer 16, ático 1ª
Tel: (93) 209 14 94 - Fax: (93) 209 37 49
E-08021 BARCELONA

Imagen corporativa. Packaging. Monografías y folletos para la industria farmacéutica, veterinaria y cosmética.

LABORATORIOS PIERRE FABRE

LABORATORIOS VITA   BAYER   LABORATORIOS IMMUNO

SAT DIVISION DE LABORATORIOS VITA

DISEÑO DE ALTURA PARA LA PRIMERA ESTACIÓN DE ESQUÍ DE ESPAÑA:

BAQUEIRA BERET *1968* DISEÑO CON PAPEL PROTAGONISTA PARA LA

PRINCIPAL EMPRESA DE MANIPULADOS DE PAPEL: UNIPAPEL *1975*

DISEÑO QUE LLEGA A TODAS PARTES PARA EL PRIMER METRO DE ESPAÑA

Y EL CUARTO DE EUROPA: METRO DE MADRID  *1982*

DISEÑO AFORTUNADO PARA EL GOBIERNO DE LAS ISLAS CANARIAS *1987*

 DISEÑO DE ALTOS VUELOS PARA LA PRIMERA COMPAÑÍA

AÉREA REGIONAL CON RESPALDO DE IBERIA  *1988*

DISEÑO DE CALIDAD PARA UNO DE LOS PRIMEROS CENTROS COMERCIALES:

*SIMAGO, AURRERÁ *1988* DISEÑO CON CRÉDITO PARA UNA DE LAS

CAJAS DE AHORROS PIONERAS EN ESPAÑA Y TERCERA EN EL RANKING

ACTUAL*  *1988* Caixa Barcelona DISEÑO ESTRELLA PARA EL PRIMER GRUPO

HOTELERO DE ESPAÑA Y TERCERO DE EUROPA *1989* Grupo Sol

DISEÑO DE LUJO PARA HOTELES CON PRESTIGIO EN TODO EL MUNDO *1989*

 Melià Hoteles DISEÑO DE FUERZA PARA EL LÍDER

s Líderes

AM&A
ARCADI MORADELL & ASOCIADOS
PROGRAMACIÓN
DE IMAGEN

PASEO BONANOVA 14 TORRE A
08022   BARCELONA
TELS. 211 51 44 211 53 04
FAX   417 89 60

VASCO DE ENERGÍA  **EVE** DISEÑO INCOMBUSTIBLE PARA LA

PRIMERA EMPRESA DE COMERCIALIZACIÓN DE DERIVADOS DEL PETRÓLEO

EN CATALUÑA DISEÑO FUNCIONAL PARA EL

LÍDER DE SERVICIOS EN LAS AUTOPISTAS ESPAÑOLAS

DISEÑO DE ENSUEÑO PARA EL LÍDER HOTELERO DE LAS AUTOPISTAS DE

ESPAÑA: HOTELES AUTOPISTA S.A.  DISEÑO DE CINCO

TENEDORES PARA EL NÚMERO UNO EN GASTRONOMÍA DE LAS AUTOPISTAS

ESPAÑOLAS. DISEÑO DE EXPERIENCIA, TRABAJO, ILUSIÓN,

CONFIANZA Y FUTURO DE UN LÍDER DEL DISEÑO DE IDENTIDAD CORPO-

RATIVA PARA TODOS NUESTROS CLIENTES.

ASÍ DISEÑAMOS LÍDERES EN ARCADI MORADELL & ASOCIADOS.

MÁS DE 20 AÑOS ESPECIALIZADOS BÁSICAMENTE EN LA PLANIFICA-

CIÓN Y EL DISEÑO DE LA IDENTIDAD CORPORATIVA PARA LAS PRINCIPA-

LES EMPRESAS, INSTITUCIONES, PRODUCTOS Y CONCEPTOS. PÓNGASE EN

CONTACTO CON NOSOTROS. LOS LÍDERES HABLAMOS EL MISMO IDIOMA.

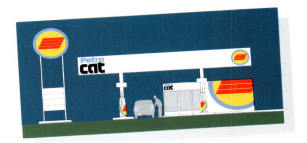

ANTONIO DIAZ & ASOCIADOS, S.A.

Avda. Dr. Federico Rubio y Galí, 67
E-28040 Madrid
Tel. 91-459 31 69
      459 34 02
Fax : 91-450 93 32

Creative direction.
Art direction.
Corporate design.
Packaging.
Illustration.

Dirección creativa.
Dirección de arte.
Diseño corporativo.
Packaging.
Ilustración.

ANTONIO DIAZ & ASOCIADOS, S.A.

Avda. Dr. Federico Rubio y Galí, 67
E-28400 Madrid
Tel. 91-459 31 69
        459 34 02
Fax : 91-450 93 32

Creative direction.
Art direction.
Corporate design.
Packaging.
Illustration.

Dirección creativa.
Dirección de arte.
Diseño corporativo.
Packaging.
Ilustración.

Tríptic

Mallorca, 1, 1.º, 9-A
Tel. 3-424 42 27
Fax : 3-425 32 48
E-08014 Barcelona

Carles Catalán
José Manuel Montero
Josep F. Roca

Una de las especialidades que nos distingue, la realización y producción de libros Promocionales, de Cocina y Recetarios.

Creación y realización de audiovisuales y videos. Creación en exclusiva de mascotas animadas para Ferias, Convenciones y Demostraciones. Salvat, Maxell, Tupperware, La Generalitat de Catalunya, ect. han confiado en nosotros.

Creatividad, Profesionalidad y
una larga trayectoria al servicio
de conocidas firmas resolviendo
sus necesidades, tanto de
diseño como de producción.

Nuestra Profesionalidad y espíritu
de servicio nos lleva a invertir
en Tecnología Punta,
para culminar un trabajo
minucioso y cuidado.

ESTUDIO DE DISEÑO GRAFICO S.A.

Castelló, 25 - 4º D - Telf.: 435 20 83 - Fax

LOGOTIPOS

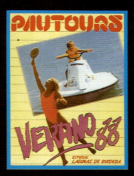

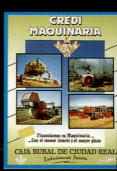

CAMPAÑAS

Diseño de Marcas
Imagen Corporativa
Diseño de Publicaciones

Folletos, Memorias, Carteles
Packaging, Ilustración y
Arte Final

20 94 - 28001 MADRID

ILUSTRACION

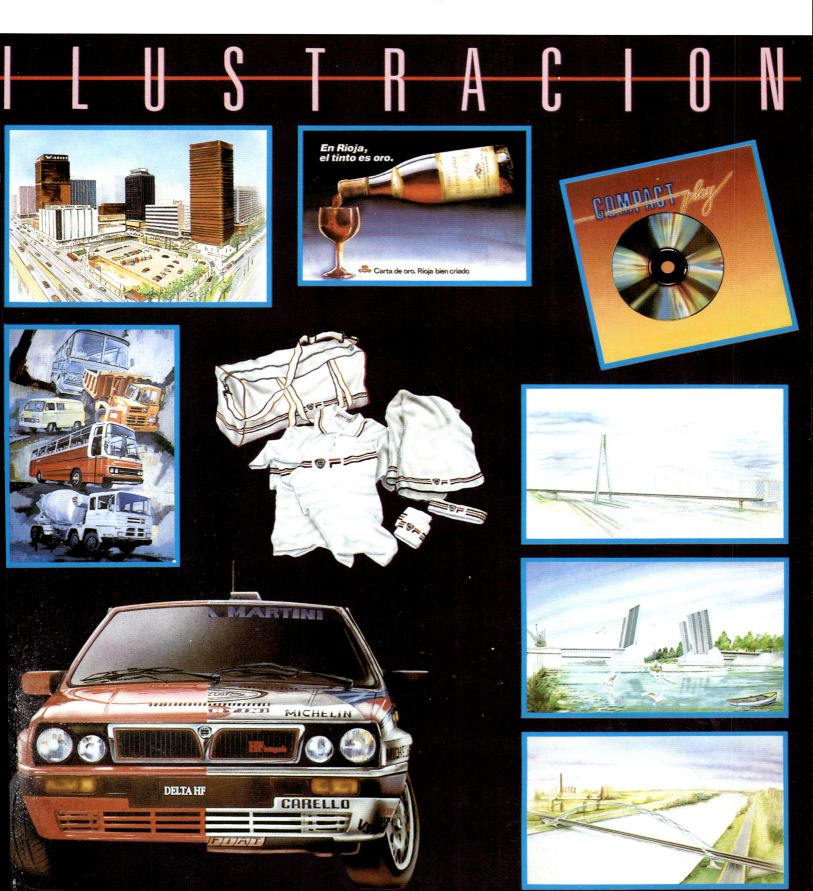

BCyM

BARCELONA CREATIVIDAD Y MEDIOS

PAU CLARIS, 97 1º - 2ª. - 08009 BARCELONA   TEL. 318 14 28 / 78 - FAX 302 06 47

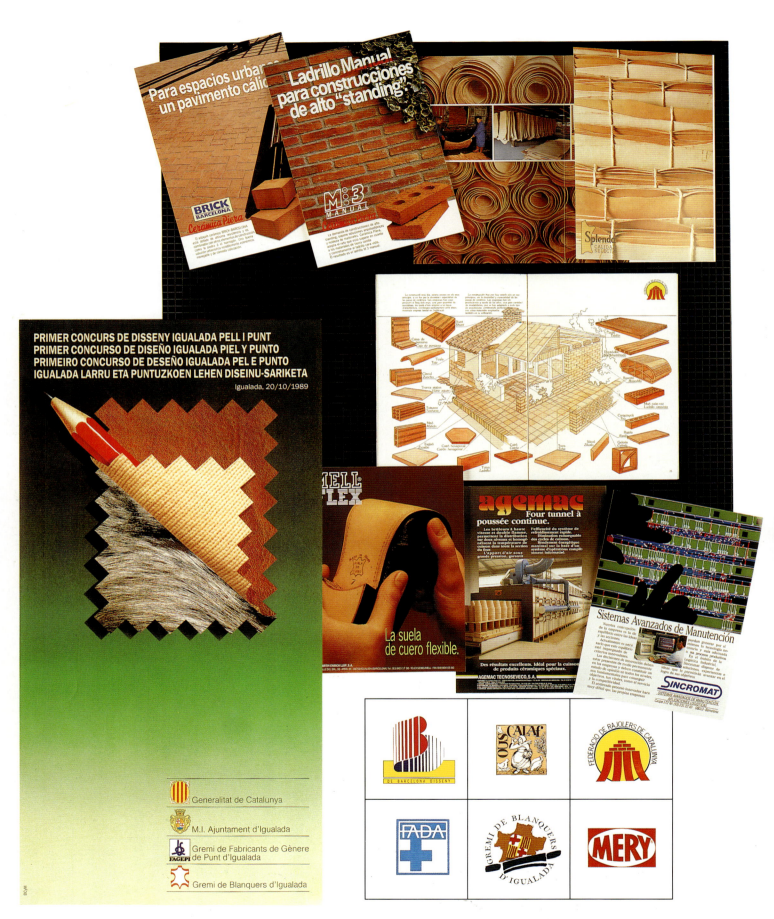

160

**CONCEPTUACION
Y REALIZACION PUBLICITARIA**
Beethoven, 15 - 7.º, 4.ª
08021 Barcelona - Spain
Tels. (93) 201 40 88 - 201 02 27
Fax (93) 209 37 43
Télex 977154 NERE-E

AR·17 es un estudio de diseño gráfico aplicado
a la publicidad. Especializado en la creación
de imagenes corporativas, packagings, ilustraciones
y todo tipo de diseños para el mundo editorial.

AR·17 is a studio of graphic design as applied
to advertising. Specialized in the creation of corporate
images, packagings, illustrations and all type of
designs for the publishing sector.

162

ESTUDIO CREATIVO DE COMUNICACION VISUAL

Imagen corporativa, logotipos, programas de identidad visual, catálogos, folletos, cartelería, señalética, edición, dirección técnica de publicaciones, ilustración, diseño industrial, imagen de marca, envoltorios, presentaciones publicitarias, decoración comercial, creación de espacios y coordinación de exposiciones.

CAMALEON

Samuel Aznar

Isidro Ferrer

Luis F. Royo

Manuel Strader

CAMALEON: Conocimiento y adaptación al medio. Paciente y pausado en sus movimientos, pero ultrarrápido a la hora de alcanzar sus objetivos. Su vista le permite descubrir distintos planos de una misma realidad.

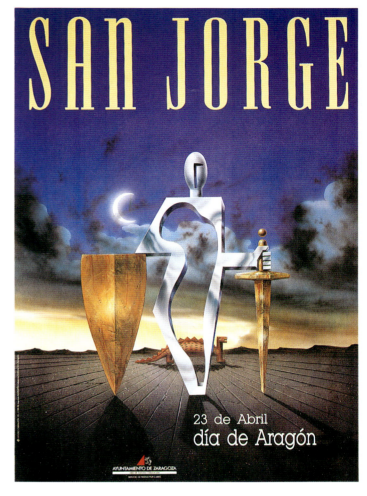

Arriba izquierda: Carpeta catálogo para un montaje audiovisual de BRIAN ENO. Arriba derecha: Cartel para la celebración del "Día de San Jorge" (Ayuntamiento de Zaragoza). Izquierda: Folleto para el montaje teatral "Tres o cuatro tubos o tubos por un tubo", del grupo PAI de animación infantil.

Al pie de estas dos páginas, diversos símbolos gráficos para actividades culturales, entidades y empresas.

Zurita, 18 - Tel. (976) 21 54 05 - Fax (976) 23 01 59 - 50001 ZARAGOZA

ZEN G.D.S.
Pedro Muguruza,6. 2ºI.
28036 MADRID
Tel:34/1/ 259 53 61• Fax:34/1/ 250 82 95

IMAGEN **C**ORPORATIVA •**M**EMORIA**S**• **P**UBLICACIONES
PUBLICIDAD(CREATIVIDAD GRAFICA)• **P**ACKAGING.
ILUSTRACION•**F**ICTICIOS• **P**RODUCCION INTEGRAL
DESDE EL CONCEPTO INICIAL AL PRODUCTO FINAL.
EQUIPO: **A**PPLE **M**ACINTOSH

CORPORATE IDENTITY• ANNUAL REPORTS•
PROMOTIONAL LITERATURE• PRESS ADVERTISSING•
POINTS OF SALE• ILLUSTRATION• FINISHED ARTWORK•
FROM INITIAL CONCEPT TO PRINTED RESULT•
APPLE MACINTOSH NETWORK•

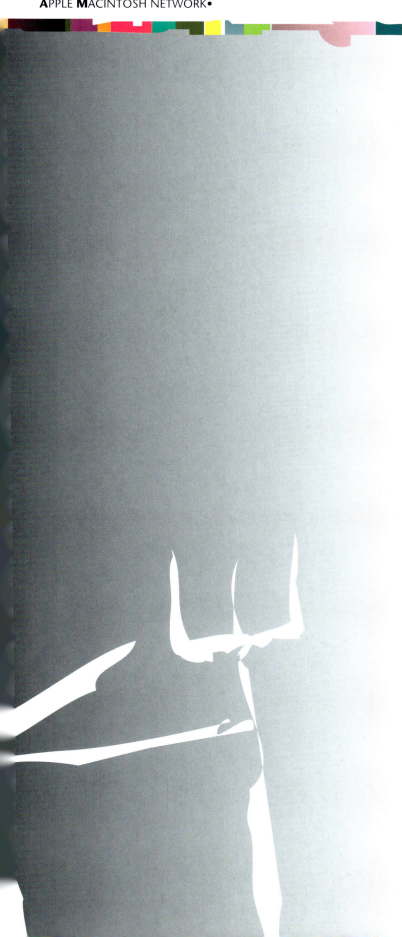

SPINTO
TELEVISION

CUSIDO &

Imagen Corporativa
Packaging
Imagen de producto
Dirección de Arte

FECSA

BASEGRAFIC

Identidad Corporativa de la Compañía Eléctrica FECSA. Aplicación en vehículos.

Corporate identity for the FECSA power company. Used on vehicles.

Identidad Corporativa de la empresa de Fotorreproducción electrónica BASEGRAFIC.

Corporate identity for the BASEGRAFIC electronic photoreproduction company.

Packaging de la gama Cola Cao crema con avellanas.

Packaging for Cola Cao's line of hazelnut butter.

Packaging de la gama de legumbres GARRIDO.

Packaging for GARRIDO's vegetable line.

CÒRSEGA 286, 2º - 2ª · TELS. 93 · 218 29 12 - 21

COMELLa

Corporate Identity
Packaging
Product Identity
Art Direction

CENTRE CULTURAL

OBRA SOCIAL DE LA CAIXA DE TERRASSA

TRAVEL PHOTO

Identidad Corporativa de la Obra Social de la Caixa de Terrassa.

Corporate identity for the Caixa de Terrassa's Comunity Projects program.

Identidad Corporativa de la cadena de tiendas de fotografía TRAVEL PHOTO.

Corporate identity for the TRAVEL PHOTO chain of photography shops.

Packaging de la gama de sopas listas para tomar en brick de KNORR.

Packaging for KNORR's "heat-and-serve" line of soups.

Identidad Corporativa de la empresa de productos de pastelería QUADRO'S. Logotipo genérico y de distintas gamas de productos.

Corporate identity for QUADRO'S, producer of bakery goods. Generic logotype and logos for the various product lines.

5 25 - FAX 237 98 21 - 08008 BARCELONA - SPAIN

AVANZANDO EN SERVICIOS GRAFICOS

Diseño Gráfico
Graphic Design

Imagen Corporativa
Corporate Identity

Diseño Editorial
Editorial Design

Ilustración
Illustration

Packaging
Packaging

Fotografía Profesional
Professional Photography

Arte Final
Final Art

Fotocomposición
Photocomposition

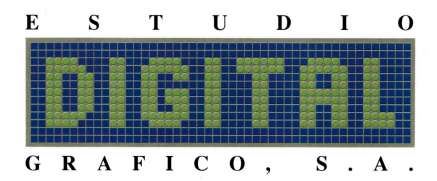

E   S   T   U   D   I   O

DIGITAL

G   R   A   F   I   C   O ,   S .   A .

KEEPING UP IN GRAPHIC PRODU'CTION

10

10 ORDENADORES

Macintosh
con Impresora Laser
y Filmadora

20

20 PERSONAS

Profesionales expertos
en comunicación visual

30

30 FIRMAS

Que confían
en nosotros

¡GRANDES!

EN MEDIOS ▪ EN EXPERIENCIA ▪ EN TECNOLOGIA
EN SERVICIOS ▪ EN CALIDAD

JOSEP MARIA VALLBONA DISSENYADOR

Móra d'Ebre 78 2.º 1.ª
E-08023 Barcelona
Tel. 93-213 46 66
Fax: 93-213 47 58

Visual communication.
Graphic design.
Corporate image.
Corporate communication design.
Applied graphic design for public places.

Comunicación visual.
Diseño gráfico.
Imagen corporativa.
Ediciones empresariales.
Imagen gráfica aplicada a espacios públicos.

Communication visuelle.
Design graphique.
Image corporative.
Editions pour entreprises.
Image graphique appliquée aux espaces publics.

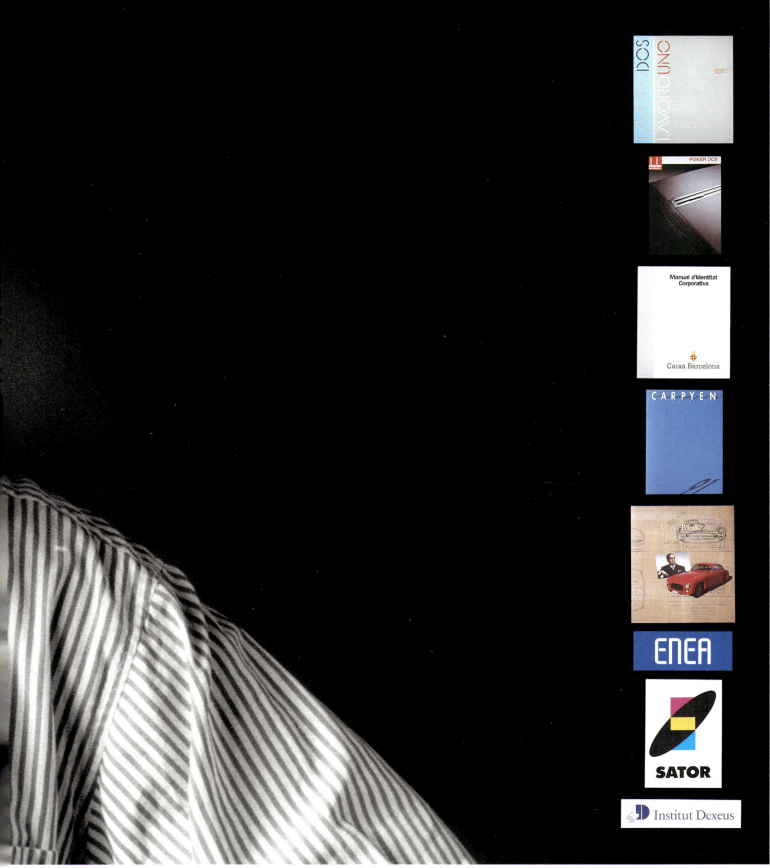

José María García Vega · DISEÑADOR GRÁFICO · Irún, 9/4 C · 28008 MADRID · 248 79 08

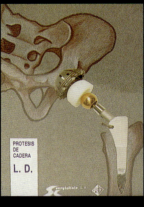

En TRAMA ART DESIGN, S.A.
resolvemos de modo integral las necesidades
de comunicación de nuestros clientes,
siguiendo de principio a fin los procesos
de diseño y realización de los trabajos,
y abarcamos todo aquello que empresas
e instituciones precisan para una comunicación
óptima y eficaz con sus públicos objetivos.

At TRAMA ART DESIGN, S.A.
we offer all-round solutions tailor-made
to our clients communication needs,
providing a close follow-up, right from
the beginning to the very end of all procedures
in designing and carrying out the job.
We cover everything companies or institutions
require in order to reach their target areas
through first-class and efficient communication.

- Diseño Gráfico
  Graphic Design
- Estudios de Identidad Corporativa
  Corporate Identity
- Estrategias de Comunicación
  Communication Strategies
- Packaging
  Packaging
- Diseño Editorial
  Editorial Design
- Ilustración
  Ilustration
- Memorias Anuales
  Annual Reports

TRAMA ART DESIGN, S.A.
Carvajal, 3 Portal 4, 2º A.
Telf.: 928 **24 53 49.** Fax: 928 23 35 62
35004 Las Palmas. ISLAS CANARIAS.

D E S I G N

Costa Canaria de **VENEGUERA**

INSTITUTO **TECNOLOGICO** DE CANARIAS

TECMA

DEBUT
[1991]

GENERAL YAGÜE Nº 10-5G 28020 MADRID

TEL-91 5972708 FAX 5972367

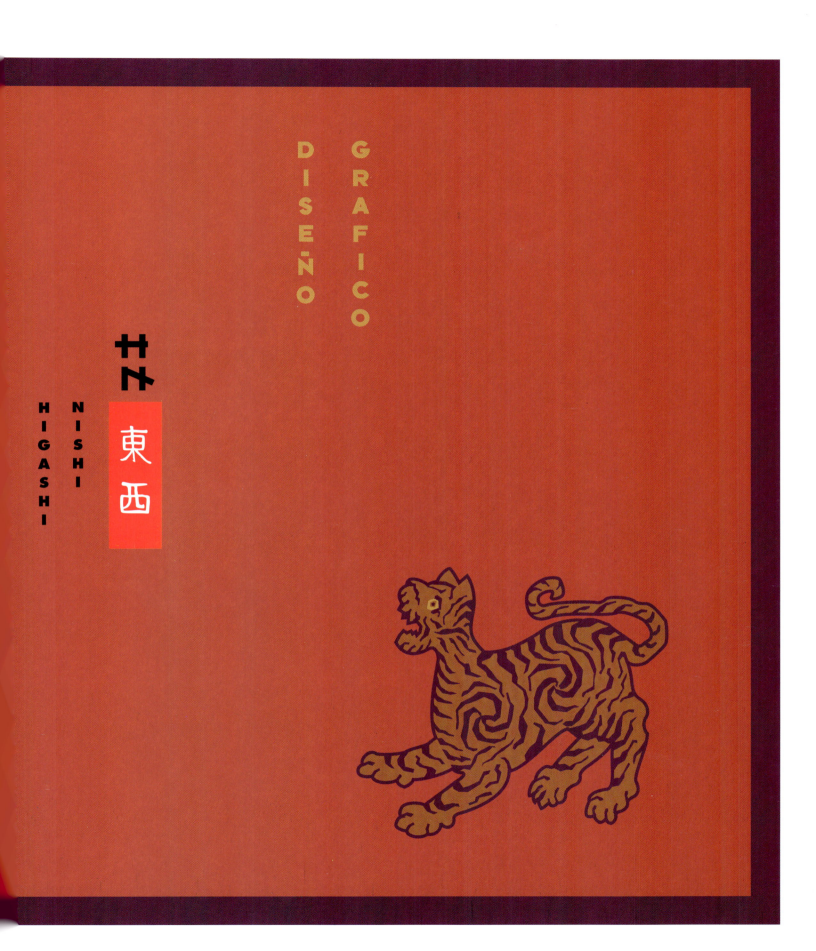

DISEÑO GRAFICO

東西

HIGASHI NISHI

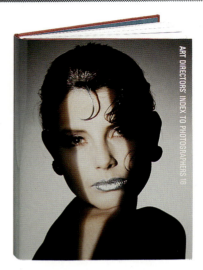
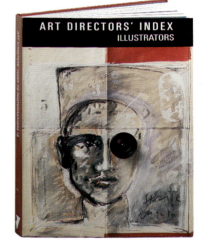
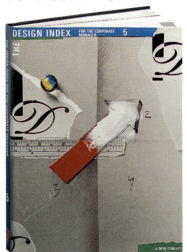

Designers

United Kingdom

Grande-Bretagne

Grossbritannien

LACKIE NEWTON LTD

13/15 Circus Lane
Edinburgh EH3 6SU
Tel. 031-220 4141
Fax : 031-220 4004

Lackie Newton is one of britain's
leading graphic design consultancies.
Working at international level
specialising in creative design and
management for the successful
marketing and positioning of
companies, products and services.

■ *Creating Commercial Advantage*

MARKETING SUPPORT

Support de ventes ■ *Apoyo a la comercialization*

CORPORATE AND BRAND I

Image de marque ■ *Identidad de la compañia y de la marca*

FINANCIAL AND CORPORAT

Documentation financiere et information sur la societe ■ *Material de informacion financiera e informacio*

PROMOTIONAL LITERATURE

Brochures publicitaires ■ *Material de propaganda*

creese learman & king

NTITIES

LITERATURE

ompania

THE YELLOW PENCIL COMPANY

2 Cosser Street
London SE1 7BU
Tel. 071-928 7801
Fax: 071-928 1419

We believe that the process of successful design does not differ from good business. It begins with applying one's energies to observation – then embark on the process of innovation.

Creemos que el proceso de éxito en el diseño no difiere de los buenos negocios. Comienza por la aplicación del esfuerzo a la observación, luego embarca en el proceso de innovación.

The Yellow Pencil Company
DESIGN CONSULTANTS

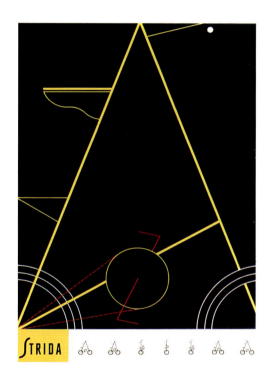

Designers

Brazil

Brésil

Brasilien

ART COMPANY DESIGN PROMOCIONAL LTDA.

Rua Bastos Pereira 454
CEP 04507 São Paulo SP
Brazil
Tel. 011-887 00 20
         885 44 80
Fax : 011-884 01 40

Agency for advertising, promotional design and visual programmes.

Principal clients :
Agro Nippo, Alpargatas, Anna Pegova, Basf, Black & Decker, Tupy Tubos and Conexões.

Agência de comunicação dirigida, design promocional e programação visual.

Principais clientes :
Agro Nippo, Alpargatas, Anna Pegova, Basf, Black & Decker, Tupy Tubos e Conexões.

Agencia de propaganda, design promocional y programación visual.

Principales clientes :
Agro Nippo, Alpargatas, Anna Pegova, Basf, Black & Decker, Tupy Tubos e Conexões.

dap design

projeto e consultoria s/c ltda

Roberto Brazil
Wanda Gomes

Rua Baluarte, 305
CEP 04549 São Paulo SP
Brasil
tel. (011) 531-3039

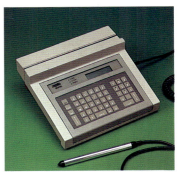

Design de Produto
Product Design
Diseño de Producto

Design Gráfico
Graphic Design
Diseño Gráfico

191

GAD - ARCHITECTURE AND DESIGN GROUP
IT IS A COMPANY THAT IN THE LAST FIVE YEARS HAS BEEN
WORKING ON THE DESIGN AS A BASIC LINE IN PROJECTS OF
COMMUNICATION AND ARCHITECTURE.
IT SHOWS A STRUCTURE OF WORK DIVIDED INTO THE AREAS OF
VISUAL COMMUNICATION, SIGN SYSTEMS, COMMERCIAL
ARCHITECTURE, PRODUCT DESIGN, EXHIBIT DESIGN
AND PHOTOGRAPHY.

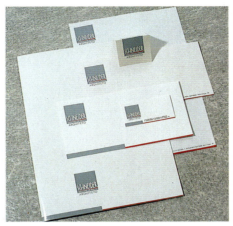

GAD - GRUPO DE ARQUITETURA E DESIGN
É UMA EMPRESA QUE HÁ CINCO ANOS VEM TRABALHANDO
O DESIGN COMO DIRETRIZ NA ELABORAÇÃO DE SEUS
PROJETOS DE COMUNICAÇÃO E ARQUITETURA.
APRESENTA UMA ESTRUTURA DE SERVIÇOS DIVIDIDA NAS
ÁREAS DE COMUNICAÇÃO VISUAL, SISTEMAS DE
SINALIZAÇÃO, ARQUITETURA COMERCIAL, DESENHO DE
PRODUTO, SISTEMAS DE EXPOSIÇÃO E FOTOGRAFIA.

RUA EUDORO BERLINK, 369 - F: (0512) 30-2874
90420 - PORTO ALEGRE - RS

RUA VISC. DE PIRAJÁ, 318/404 - F: (021) 521-5095
22410 - RIO DE JANEIRO - RJ

BRASIL

192

Designers

Chile
Chili
Chile

EDICIONES HERNAN GARFIAS LTDA.

Almirante Pastene 232
Providencia
Santiago
Chile
Tel.   46 55 95
        223 57 38
Fax : 56-2-46 55 95

We are a group specialized in the design and the edition of magazines, books, catalogues, and annual reports.

Among our clients :
Editorial Los Andes, Editorial Lord Cochrane, La Chilena Consolidada, Ripley, Acop, Cecinas Winter, Nike, Echicolit and Revista Diseño.

Grupo de especialistas en diseño y ediciones de revistas, libros, catálogos y memorias anuales.

Algunos clientes :
Editorial Los Andes, Editorial Lord Cochrane, La Chilena Consolidada, Ripley, Acop, Cecinas Winter, Nike, Echicolit y Revista Diseño.

Un Estudio de Diseñadores dedicados a innovar e implementar nuevas posibilidades de diseño para su Empresa.

Nuestro compromiso es abrirle alternativas de negocios, creando la imagen de su Empresa e inventando nuevos productos.

Regina Humeres 230
Santiago - Chile
Tel. 37 22 55
37 97 19
Fax: 052-372255

Proyecto:
amiento Hall de cajeros
Cliente: Banco Santander

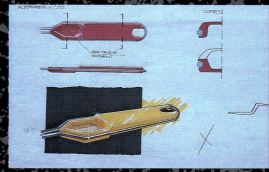

Proyecto:
Línea de Coladores
de Exportación
Rendering:
Desarrollo de Asas para
Línea de Coladores
Cliente: ILKO

Proyecto:
Línea de Etiquetas
oducto de Exportación
nte: Pesquera Eicomar

Designers

Venezuela
Venezuela
Venezuela

MONTANA GRAFICA DISEÑO 198-199

Designers

L'étude de dessin de Montana Gráfica se réfère à un atelier d'art complet, spécialisé en matière de dessin graphique et structurel pour emballages, logos et illustrations.

Faisant partie intégrante du groupe industriel Corimon, lequel s'adonne à la production de produits chimiques, de peintures, d'emballages et d'aliments, Montana Gráfica semble être une compagnie vénézuelienne leader en étuis et emballages flexibles.

Die Planungsabteilung von Montana Grafica spezialisiert sich auf graphisches und strukturelles Dessin für Verpackung, (Logos), und illustriertes Werk.

Montana Grafica gehört zur Corimongruppe, diese Gruppe steht im Zusammenhang mit Chemischen Erzeugnissen, Farbstoffen, Verpackung und Lebensmitteln. Montana Grafica spielt die Führungsrolle bei der Herstellung von biegsamem Packmaterial in Venezuela.

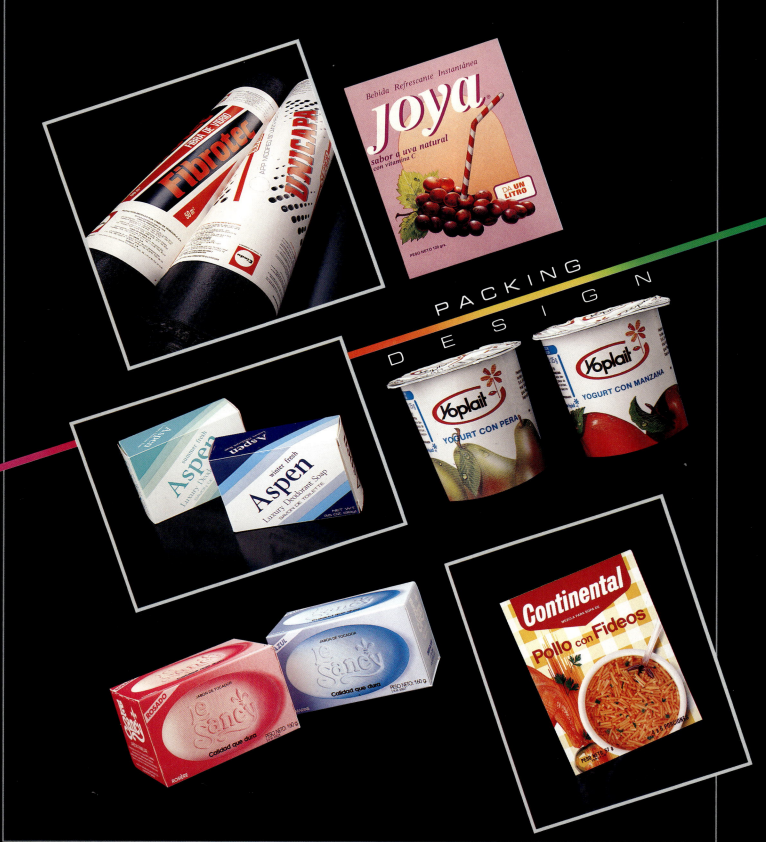

PACKING DESIGN

Montana Grafica's design studio is a complete art department specialized in graphic and structural design for packaging, logos and illustrations. Being part of the Corimon industrial group with activities in Chemical products, paints, packaging and food, Montana Grafica is the leading Venezuelan folding box and flexible packaging company.

Montana Gráfica, Av. Ppal. Boleíta Norte, Caracas 1060-A. Venezuela. Tel: (02) 238/09/44 Fax (02) 35/39/85

If it's creative, it's bound to be on the RotoVision list.

PHOTOGRAPHY

ART DIRECTORS' INDEX TO PHOTOGRAPHERS
STOCK PHOTO INTERNATIONAL
AMERICAN SHOWCASE — PHOTOGRAPHY
COMMUNICATION ARTS — PHOTOGRAPHY
CONCEPTUAL PEOPLE PHOTOGRAPHY
CONCEPTUAL STILL LIFE PHOTOGRAPHY
CRETE DI SIENA
STOCK WORKBOOK

ILLUSTRATION

ART DIRECTORS' INDEX TO ILLUSTRATORS
AMERICAN SHOWCASE — ILLUSTRATION
AIRBRUSH ART IN JAPAN
COMMUNICATION ARTS — ILLUSTRATION
FIGURE DRAWING FOR FASHION
FLOWER ILLUSTRATION
SOCIETY OF AMERICAN ILLUSTRATORS

CORPORATE IDENTITY

CORPORATE SHOWCASE
CORPORATE SOURCE
GRAPHIS ANNUAL REPORTS

NATIONAL MULTI-CATEGORY

ADI ESPAÑA
AMERICAN SHOWCASE — SET
CREATIVE SOURCE AUSTRALIA
CREATIVE SOURCE CANADA
SINGLE IMAGE
THE WORKBOOK
TALENTO

ADVERTISING & EDITORIAL CAMPAIGNS

ADVERTISING DESIGN IN JAPAN
ADVERTISING'S TEN BEST OF THE DECADE
ART DIRECTORS ANNUAL
COMMUNICATION ARTS — ADVERTISING
DOSSIER AGENCES
EPICA — EUROPEAN ADVERTISING
GOTCHA!
JAHRBUCH
ONE SHOW
VENUS

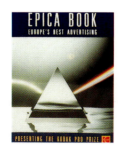

GRAPHIC DESIGN & PACKAGING

THE DESIGN INDEX FOR THE CORPORATE MANAGER
BEST LOGOS & SYMBOLS
BEST LETTERHEADS & BUSINESS CARDS
BRAND IDENTITY
COMMUNICATION ARTS — DESIGN
GRAPHIC DESIGN IN JAPAN
GRAPHIC DESIGN USA
GRAPHIS PUBLICATION
GRAPHIS LOGOS
GRAPHIS LETTERHEADS
THE GREEN BOOK (Designing to Save the Environment)
ICOGRADA — GRAPHIC DESIGN WORLD VIEWS
KOREAN MOTIF BOOKS
ONTWERPEN IN OPDRACHT
   (Annnual of Dutch Designers Association)
PUBLICATION DESIGN ANNUAL
PRINT REGIONAL DESIGN ANNUAL
ROCK, SCISSORS, PAPER
STORKS & BONDS
TYPOGRAPHY
WORLD GRAPHIC DESIGN NOW 1 — POSTERS
WORLD GRAPHIC DESIGN NOW 2 — ADVERTISING
WORLD GRAPHIC DESIGN NOW 3 — PACKAGING
WORLD GRAPHIC DESIGN NOW 4 — CORPORATE IDENTITY
WORLD GRAPHIC DESIGN NOW 5 — EDITORIAL
WORLD GRAPHIC DESIGN NOW 6 — COMPUTER GRAPHICS

COMMERCIAL SPACE, ENVIRONMENTAL AND INTERIOR DESIGN

ABITARE
ARCHITECTURAL DESIGN COLLABORATORS
DISPLAY AND COMMERCIAL SPACE DESIGNS IN JAPAN
DIRECTORY OF INTERIOR DESIGNERS
ELEMENTS & TOTAL CONCEPT
   OF URBAN PAVEMENT DESIGN
ELEMENTS & TOTAL CONCEPT
   OF URBAN WATERSCAPE DESIGN
INTERIOR BEST SELECTION
RESORT HOTELS
SHOP DESIGNING
SHOWCASE OF INTERIOR DESIGN

PRODUCTS

CROPPER
MINI-PRO PORTABLE LIGHT BOX
MAXI-PRO PORTABLE LIGHT BOX

A World Class Creative Collection

The RotoVision list goes from strength to strength. Our ever expanding range includes the leading annual sourcebooks and reference material of the visual communications industry.

These are the titles you're looking for. Across the categories, you'll find the work of the leading organizations and individuals that are setting new trends in their respective areas. The Best of the Best.

ROTOVISION

ROTOVISION SA   Route Suisse 9, CH–1295 Mies, Switzerland · Tel. (0)22-755 30 55 · Telex 419 246 rovi ch · Fax (0)22-755 40 72

Designers

Canada

Canada

Kanada

Cranwell & Pietrasiak
DESIGN ASSOCIATES

Annual Reports

Corporate & Product Identity

Packaging

9 Hazelton Avenue

Third Floor

Toronto, Canada

M5R 2E1

PH: 1-(416) 975-1699

FX: 1-(416) 975-4031

**Society of
Graphic Designers
of Canada**

**Société
des Graphistes
du Canada**

The Society of Graphic Designers of
Canada (GDC) is the only
national association of professional
graphic designers in Canada.

Find out about the benefits of
joining the GDC by contacting your
local chapter today.

Atlantic
P.O. Box 1533, Station M
Halifax, NS B3J 2Y3
(902) 425-0015

Ottawa
P.O. Box 2245, Station D
Ottawa, ON K1P 5W4
(613) 238-7108

Ontario (Toronto)
Adelaide Street P.O., Box 813
Adelaide St. E., Toronto, ON M5C 2K1
(416) 420-6962

Alberta
c/o University of Alberta
Department of Art and Design
3-98, Fine Arts Bldg.
Edmonton, AB T6G 2C9
(403) 492-3456

Manitoba
c/o Circle Design Inc.
601-63 Albert Street,
Winnipeg, MB R3B 1G4
(204) 943-3693

British Columbia
VMPO, P.O. Box 3626
Vancouver, BC V6B 3X6
(604) 254-3210

DANIEL JALBERT, **JARS DESIGN INC.** 10, RUE ONTARIO OUEST, BUREAU 903, MONTREAL (QUEBEC)   H2X 1Y6   (514) 844-0530 FAX (514) 844-6002

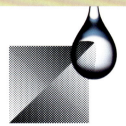

IDENTIFICATION VISUELLE ET PRODUCTION

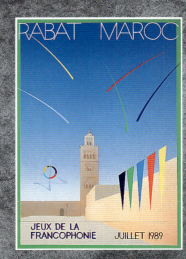

RABAT MAROC

JEUX DE LA
FRANCOPHONIE · JUILLET 1989

DENISE FALARDEAU

*Solidaires
dans
l'action*

RICHARD ADAMS
Galeries

BACCHUS

QUALITÉ EN PRIOR
DOMTAR

Photos: l'ami Jac Mat

LEGOUPIL
COMMUNICATIONS

424 RUE GUY

BUREAU 200

MONTRÉAL, QC.

H3J 1S6

FAX : 939-3628

TÉL. : 939-3379

REACTOR ART & DESIGN LTD.

51 CAMDEN STREET TORONTO CANADA

TEL (416) 362 1913

FAX (416) 362 6356

EFFECTIVE

VISUAL

COMMUNICATION

BATA IN-STORE RETAIL ADVERTISING

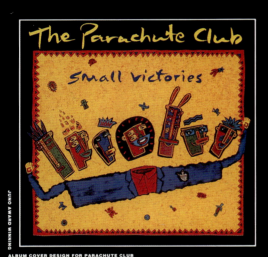

JUNO AWARD WINNING

ALBUM COVER DESIGN FOR PARACHUTE CLUB

> **66**
>
> *Reactor brings art out of studios, lofts, garrets and galleries into magazines, retail advertising, sports promotions, tv commercials and mass merchandising*
>
> **99**

APPLIED ARTS QUARTERLY

A PRIVATE LABEL GRAPHICS

ROOTS ATHLETICS LOGO

GRAPHIC DESIGN

ILLUSTRATION

CORPORATE

CULTURAL

RETAIL

EDITORIAL

VISUAL IDENTITY

ADVERTISING

MERCHANDISING

PRIVATE LABEL

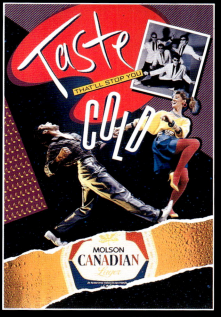

MOLSON CANADIAN AD CAMPAIGN

CLIENT: MACLAREN ADVERTISING

DEMANDS **BOLD** **SOLUTIONS**

TORONTO BLUE JAYS SCOREBOOK MAGAZINE

COMPLETE IDENTITY DESIGN PROGRAM FOR CANPAR DELIVERY SERVICE, A DIVISION OF CP TRUCKS

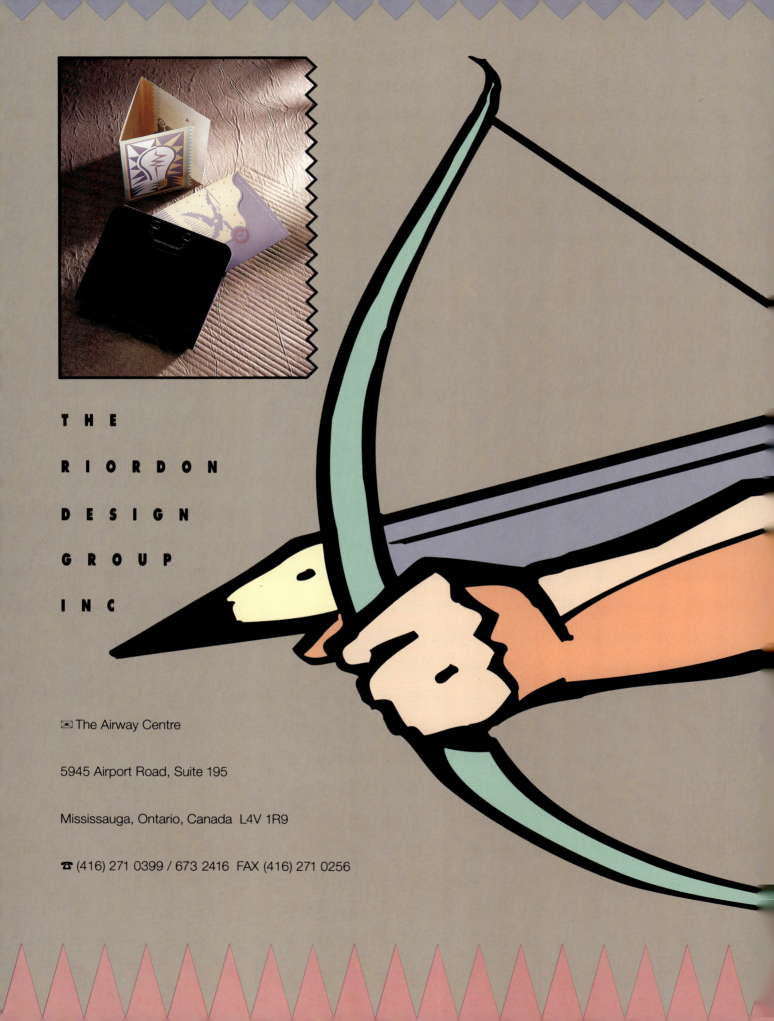

THE RIORDON DESIGN GROUP INC

✉ The Airway Centre

5945 Airport Road, Suite 195

Mississauga, Ontario, Canada L4V 1R9

☎ (416) 271 0399 / 673 2416 FAX (416) 271 0256

Woodwin
Renovations Contractors

Woodwin handles all stages of development and construction. Working for the home and institutional market, Woodwin completes its assignments from concept development through to the finishing touches.

The Canadian Autoworkers

On December 1, 1984, the Canadian UAW Council approved a recommendation from UAW Director for Canada Bob White that unless the UAW in Canada was able to achieve complete autonomy within the International Union, two separate and distinct unions should be structured, one in the U.S. and one in Canada.

National Forest Congress

The National Forest Congress was planned to act as a catalyst for the development of policies to meet the challenges facing Canada's forest sector through the Eighties and the Nineties, and into the 21st century.

Toronto
Arts Against Apartheid
Festival Foundation

The issue of apartheid in South Africa first received attention in 1962 when Nelson Mandela was imprisoned on charges of conspiracy and sabotage. The Festival was planned to use public support, to encourage corporate support, government endorsement and political action.

THE
PAY EQUITY
COMMISSION

Ron Kaplansky believes that good design requires time and communication with the client at the concept stage. His sensitivity and intuition, combined with a solid background in graphic design, direct you to the best visual approach for your needs.

You'll exchange ideas and discuss concrete visual suggestions. When the approach has been agreed upon, Ron will complete all phases of production including printing supervision, if required.

Ron's work, which has included annual reports, educational displays, posters, large and small publications, and advertisements, is distinguished by its simplicity and clarity.

The Pay Equity Commission

As of January 1, 1988 employers in Ontario are legally bound to set up pay equity plans to make sure that their salary and wage scales are based on the value of work performed – regardless of the sex of the person doing the work.

Imperial Pipe Corporation

Imperial Pipe Corporation is a manufacturer of plastic piping. It transforms Low, Medium and High Density Polyethylene Polypropylene and ABS resins into finished pressure piping.

Metro World 1991

Metro World 1991 is being planned as a coordinated response to the urgent environmental issues arising in world metropolises. Our ability to respond to these urban challenges will determine, in large part, the global quality of life for the 21st century.

Ron Kaplansky
Graphic Designer
R.K. Studios Limited
309 Wellesley Street East
Toronto, Ontario
M4X 1H2

Tel: (416) 964-6991
Fax: (416) 964-8900

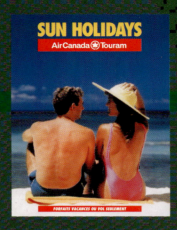

**Wolf Schell & Associates Inc. ist eine Design Agentur
zu deren Hauptarbeitsgebieten neben der Entwicklung von
Corporate Identity Programmen auch die Konzeption und
Durchführung aller kommunikativen Massnahmen gehören.**

1220 Mackay, Montréal, H3G 2H4, tél 514 935 7098, fax 514 935 8794

Wolf Schell+Associates Inc.

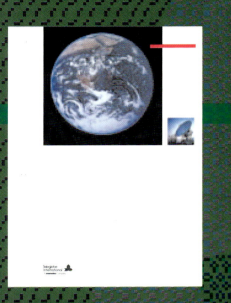

Wolf Schell et associés se spécialise dans l'image et la communication corporative. Que vos besoins relève de design, direction artistique ou d'illustration, nous avons l'expertise pour y répondre de façon intégrale.

Wolf Schell & Associates Inc. specializes in corporate image development and visual communications for business. We provide turnkey service for needs analysis, concept and design with innovative computer assisted production technology.

IRIS

Canada direct

LE MOT DESSINÉ INC.
COMMUNICATION GRAPHIQUE

THE EXPERIENCE TO IMPLEMENT INGENUITY, CREATIVITY, IMAGIN◆TION, PROFESSIONAL THOROUGHNESS AND TECHNICAL SUPPORT

LE SAVOIR-FAIRE MIS AU SERVICE DE L'INGÉNIOSITÉ, DE L'IMAGIN◆TION, DE LA RIGUEUR PROFESSIONNELLE ET DE L'AIDE TECHNIQUE

5890, AVENUE MONKLAND ◆ BUREAU 401 ◆ MONTRÉAL (QUÉBEC) CANADA ◆ H4A 1G2 ◆ TÉLÉCOPIEUR (514) 485.3034
TÉLÉPHONE (514) **485.1800**

Designers

United States
Etats-Unis
Vereinigte Staaten

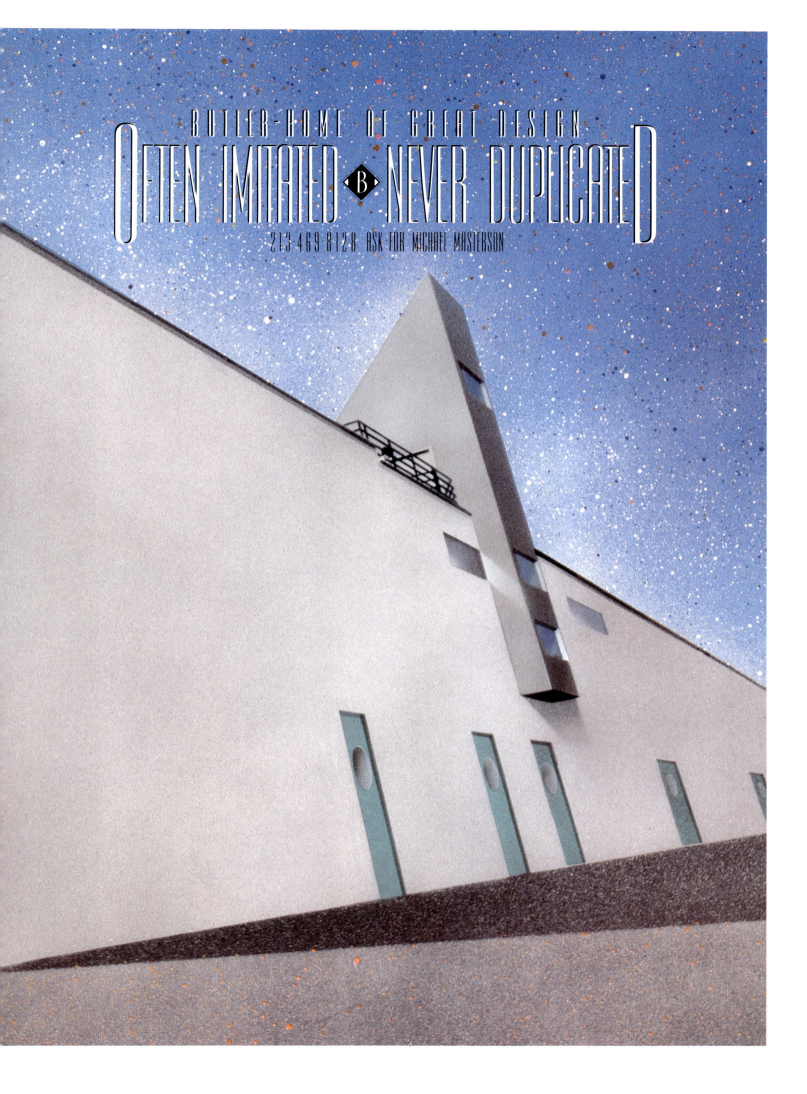

BUTLER-HOME OF GREAT DESIGN

OFTEN IMITATED ◈ B ◈ NEVER DUPLICATED

213·469·8128 ASK FOR MICHAEL MASTERSON

BLACKDOG

415.331.DAWG

MARGO CHASE DESIGN   2255 BANCROFT AVE   LA CA 90039   213 668 1055   FAX 213 668 2470

 olly Dickens designs lettering for TV, movies, print advertising, logos, packaging and promotions for most of the top 50 advertisers and some small hot ones.

American
ANTHEM

MOVIE TITLE · UNIVERSAL PICTURES

RETAIL LOGO · FLORIDA CLOTHING STORE

It's how
Steak
Is Done.

T.V. SUPER · NABISCO

RRRuffles have RRRidges

T.V. SUPER · FRITO LAY

The Designers

CORPORATE IDENTITY · DESIGN FIRM

CORPORATE LOGO · ENTERTAINMENT PROMOTIONS

NEW ANGLES

RETAIL SIGNAGE · MARSHALL FIELDS

CORPORATE IDENTITY · CHICAGO HAIR SALON

ENCICLOPEDIA
HISPÁNICA

BOOK TITLE · ENCYCLOPEDIA BRITANNICA

Dae Julie
World Class Candy.™

CORPORATE LOGO · GOURMET CANDY COMPANY

DOGLIGHT
STUDIOS

RONALD DUNLAP

TONY HONKAWA

(213) 222-1928

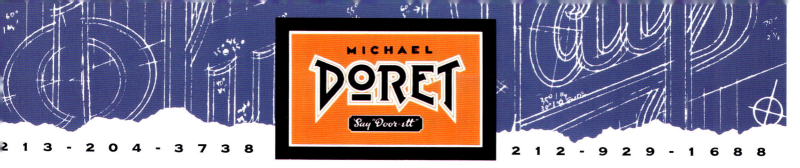

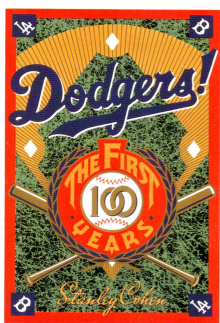

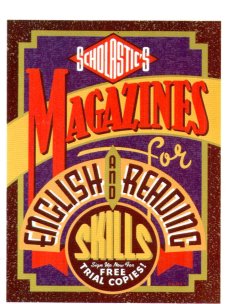

STAN EVENSON DESIGN

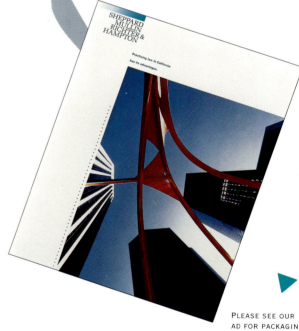

PLEASE SEE OUR
AD FOR PACKAGING
AND POINT OF SALE
DISPLAY UNDER
PRINTING SERVICES IN
THE WORKBOOK
DIRECTORY.

4445 OVERLAND AVENUE CULVER CITY, CA 90230

CREATIVE 213.204.1995   SALES 213.204.0941   FAX 213.204.4879

DEAN GERRIE DESIGN

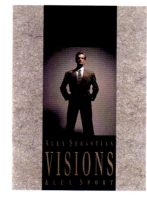

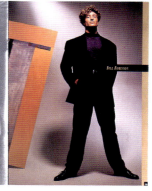

DEAN GERRIE DESIGN, INC.

TELEPHONE 714/647-9488

FAX 714/647-0193

TIM GIRVIN DESIGN, INC.

The Fifth Floor
1601 Second Avenue
Seattle, Washington 98101

206.623.7808
Fax: 206.340.1837

Represented in New York
by Renard Represents

212.490.2450

Typographic Treatments,
Illustration, Identity
Development, Promotion,
Brochures, Packaging,
Store Design,
Conference and
Exhibit, Signage,
Environmental Graphics

Bloomingdale's
Hasbro, Inc.
Macy's
Microsoft
Newsweek
Nintendo
Paramount Pictures
Simpson Paper Co.
Spectrum Foods International
Town & Country
United Airlines

Almost AN ANGEL

ALDUS

DESIGN TEAM

DAY

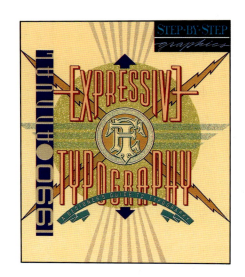

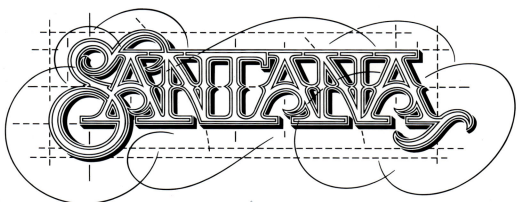

SANTANA: FROM AN ORIGINAL DESIGN BY BOB VENOSA

232

KELLY HUME
D E S I G N
Telephone/Fax
818·793·8344

Logos and Lettering for Advertising,
Entertainment and Corporate Identity

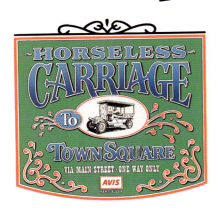

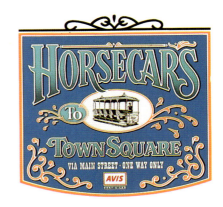

STUDIO
(206) 323.8256

ISKRA

EXPRESSIVE

LETTERING &

TYPOGRAPHIC

DESIGN

Blush Chablis

BAD INFLUENCE

The SHUMWAY

BOCADILLOS
SWEET FLOUR TORTILLA TREATS

NATIVE ORIGINS

ISKRA JOHNSON
Typographic solutions for
logos, book and film titles,
headlines and packaging.
Clients include: Anheuser
Busch, Neutrogena, AT&T,
Westin Hotels, McDonald's,
MGM/UA, Bantam Books,
Eddie Bauer, Penguin USA,
and Polaroid. A portfolio of
additional lettering styles is
available on request.

Represented by:
MUNRO GOODMAN
Midwest and East Coast
Phone: (312) 321.1336

SUSAN TRIMPE
West Coast and Publishing
Phone: (206) 728.1300

FAX in studio.

Stamping Our History

KANE

Vin Rosé

Amethyst

234

Fumé Blanc

Veneto's
A COFFEE BAR

EXPRESSIVE
LETTERING &
TYPOGRAPHIC
DESIGN

SKRA

THE
NIGHTMARE
PEOPLE

Pinot Noir

Represented by:
MUNRO GOODMAN
Midwest and East Coast
Phone: (312) 321.1336

SUSAN TRIMPE
West Coast and Publishing
Phone: (206) 728.1300

FAX in studio.

CIVIC
LIGHT
OPERA

Market-Direct

EDDIE BAUER
All Week Long®
SUMMER 1990

koalas

Perestroika

Letters from Home

DESIGN AND ILLUSTRATION: RON LARSON

ILLUSTRATION: RON LARSON

ILLUSTRATION: RON LARSON

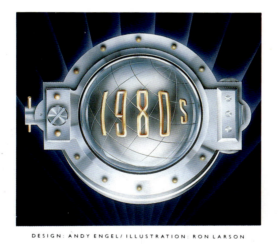

DESIGN: ANDY ENGEL/ ILLUSTRATION: RON LARSON

DESIGN: ANDY ENGEL/ ILLUSTRATION: RON LARSON

DESIGN: L-SHAPE/ ILLUSTRATION: RON LARSON

DESIGN: PAUL PASCRELLA

R O N   L A R S O N

[2 1 3] · 4 6 5 · 8 4 5 1

IRE!" CRIED A LILTING VOICE. The Prince of Promotion turned 'round.

And beheld the fairest lass he had ever seen. It was the Maid of Marketing.

The Prince knew it was the  of a lifetime.

And he immediately sought to win her hand.

He courted her at  the most romantic

refuge in the land.

But alas, the Maid of Marketing was not pleased.

"I want some real  she cried.

So the Prince took her to **THE RANCH** to ride the fastest steed in the Kingdom.

But nothing would melt the stubborn Maid's heart –

not even the Royal Family **TIARA**

"I need professional help," thought the Prince in despair.

And he called

BONNIE LEAH Lettering and Design

She helped him create *A Campaign* of love

that was hailed throughout the Kingdom.

From *Home & Castle* to *Princess Bride* magazine, the Maid of Marketing was beseeched by the Prince's love.

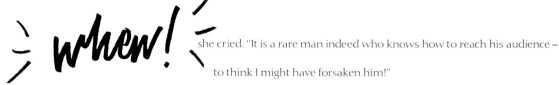 she cried. "It is a rare man indeed who knows how to reach his audience –

to think I might have forsaken him!"

The Prince and the Maid were married at once. And she became the Princess of Marketing and Promotion.

Bonnie Leah Lettering and Design

Classical and Contemporary Lettering Design

714·752·7820   FAX 714·833·3367   1801 Dove Street   Suite 104   Newport Beach   California   92660

Letter·Perfect

6606 Soundview Drive
Gig Harbor, WA 98335
(206) 851-5158

Lettering · Logos · Type Design

lettering artists: Garrett Boge, Janet Baker
Additional samples and estimates
returned overnight or same day via fax.

BRUSH

FORMAL

CASUAL

DRAWN

DIGITAL

Collateral Literature

Corporate and Retail Graphics

Displays and Exhibits

Annual Reports

Packaging

M SQUARED DESIGN

10401 Jefferson Boulevard
Culver City, CA 90232-1928
(213) 202-0140 FAX 202-8219

A MultiMedia Group Company

Our official position on the state of the art:

A little to the left.
A little up and to the right.
Perfectly centered.
Squared top and bottom.
And of course, on time.

MECHANICAL PRODUCTION ART SERVICE

Mechanical and Computerized Production Art and Inking/MAC Literate: Quark Express, Freehand, Illustrator
3958 Ince Boulevard/Culver City/CA 90232/Phone: 213-837-1904/Fax: 213-837-0907

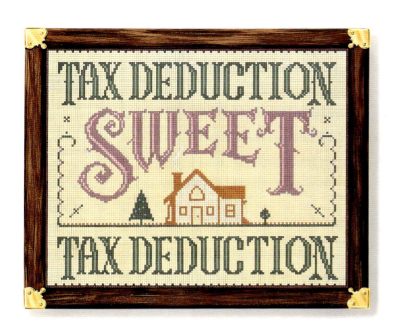

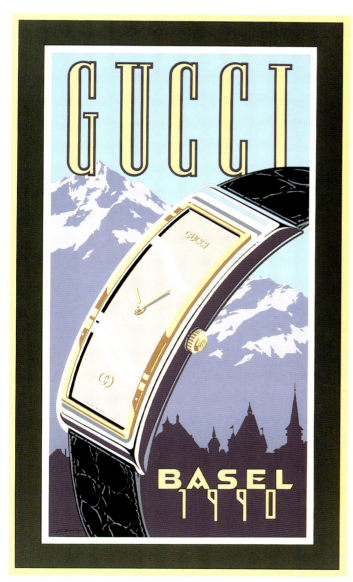

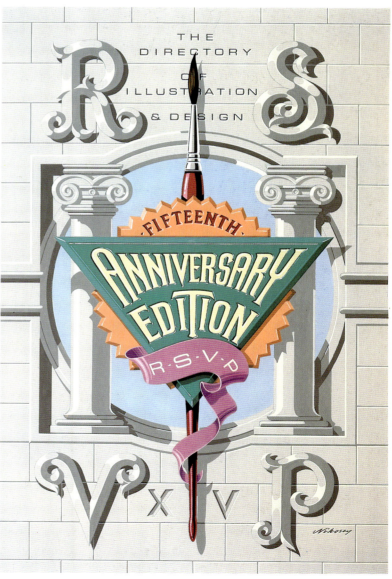

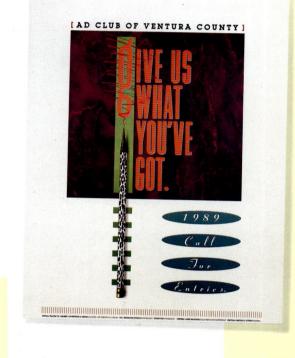

Thank you
from the bottom of
our hearts.

Anything
Your
Mind
Imagines...

ACAPULCO

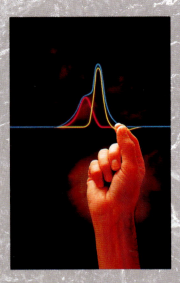

BASEBALL
1990 EDITION

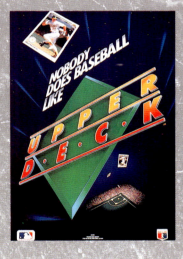

DESIGN

AUDIO VISUAL

LOGO TREATMENTS

MOTION CONTROL

SPECIAL EFFECTS

SCAN OPTICS

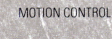

Optical Artists
308 South Catalina Ave.
Redondo Beach, California
90277

TEL: 213.376.8859
FAX: 213.376.8064

Special Effects for Design

Fax your layout for a quotation.

243

PHONE

3958 INCE BOULEVARD • CULVER CITY • CALIFORNIA 90232

Smithkline Beecham

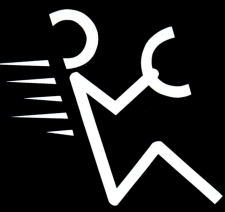

Volkswagen

Univision

Tapsa/N.W. Ayer

Harper & Row

DC Comics

Tapsa/N.W. Ayer

design art direction digital effects animation

213 456 7569

1033
S. ORLANDO
AVENUE
LOS ANGELES
CALIFORNIA
90035
213.655.7734*
FAX 213.655.2067
*REPRESENTED BY MARTHA WIHNYK

Sigwart
D E S I G N

CREATIVE DESIGN, LETTERING & ILLUSTRATION FOR
ADVERTISING, ENTERTAINMENT, PACKAGING & PROMOTIONS.

1. THRU 4. TRADEMARK & GRAPHICS FOR MAUI DOG SPORTSWEAR.

5. LETTERING FOR GIORGIO RED PROMOTION.
6. LOGO FOR ROCK & ROLL PROMOTER.
7. PRIVATE SPEEDBOAT LETTERING.
8. GRAPHIC FOR SECURITY PACIFIC BANK PROMOTION.

9. AMUSEMENT PARK SIGNAGE & TRADEMARK.
10. CENTENNIAL ROSE BOWL GRAPHIC.
11. YAMAHA SPORTING GOODS LOGO.
12. LOGO/SIGNATURE FOR TV PRODUCTION CO.

13. THEME PARK LOGO/GRAPHIC.
14. COMPUTER COMPANY TRADEMARK.

1.

5.

GIORGIO

6.

10.

2.

11.

7.

LIVINGSTON 5

12.

3.

8.

13.

4.

9.

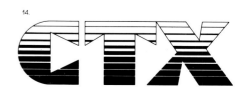

14.

DOGMEAT.

At least that's what our clients thought about these designs. Thank goodness there were other logos in the presentation they liked. And bought. If you'd like to see those, call 213.395.3939 for our full-color, dog-free brochure and portfolio.

248

SHIFFMAN YOUNG DESIGN GROUP *7421 Beverly Boulevard Suite 4 Los Angeles California 90036 213 930.1816*

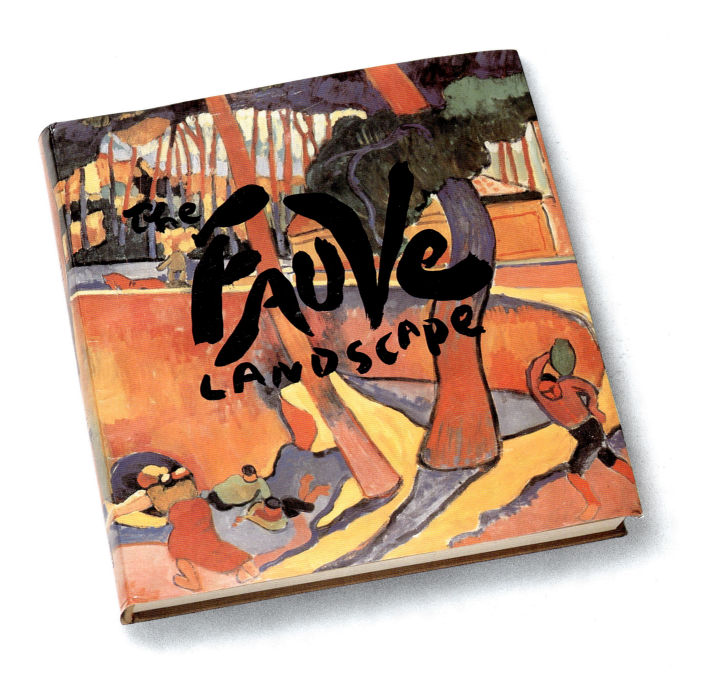

Client: Los Angeles
County
Museum of
Art

John Stevens
516.579.5352
Fax: 516.735.6535

John Stevens transforms ordinary verbal symbols into extraordinary visual statements... characters with the character to speak for themselves. There are many applications for John Stevens' work, such as...logotypes, trademarks, titles, book jackets, posters, film and packaging.

Atlantic Records
Barrons
Canon
HBO
Headliners
James River
Lucasfilm
Newsday
N.Y. Public Library
N.Y. Magazine
Time Inc.
Random House
Revlon

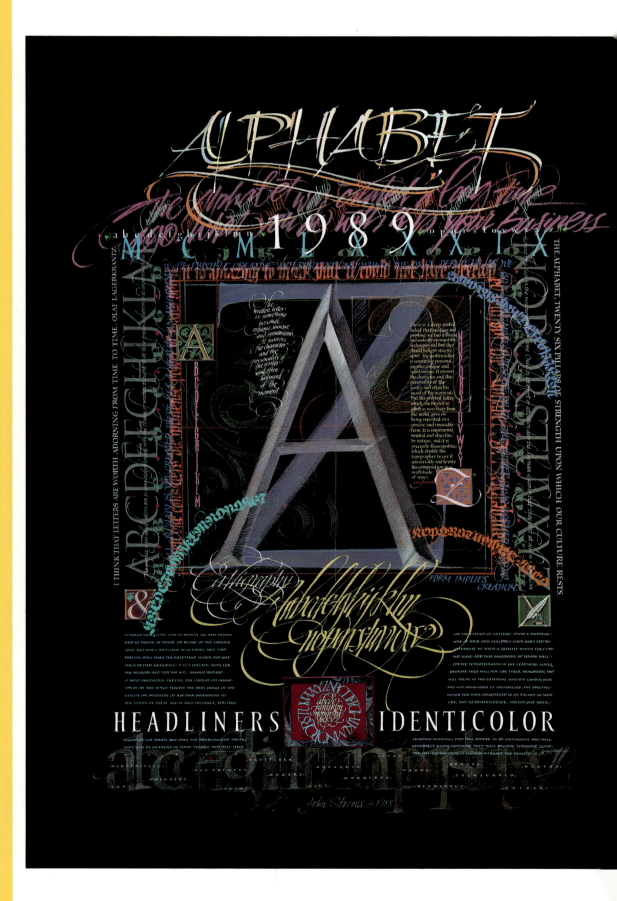

TRACY CHAPMAN

Anita Baker

A Kidder, Peabody Broker

Macy's Flower Show
1 9 8 9

Undeniably Billy

Heartland

BANGKOK

Lon Po Po

A RED·RIDING HOOD STORY FROM CHINA

ED YOUNG

BABYTALK

John Stevens
516.579.5352
Fax: 516.735.6535

John Stevens transforms ordinary verbal symbols into extraordinary visual statements... characters with the character to speak for themselves. There are many applications for John Stevens' work, such as...logotypes, trademarks, titles, book jackets, posters, film and packaging.

Atlantic Records
Barrons
Canon
HBO
Headliners
James River
Lucasfilm
Newsday
N.Y. Public Library
N.Y. Magazine
Time Inc.
Random House
Revlon

SHARKFIN

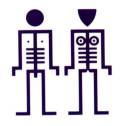

a x i s

Design and Art Direction

JAY VIGON

Tel. 213 654 4771 or 654 4996
Fax 213 654 1915

252

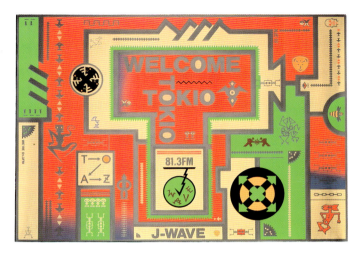

Design and Art Direction

JAY VIGON

Tel. 213 654 4771 or 654 4996
Fax 213 654 1915

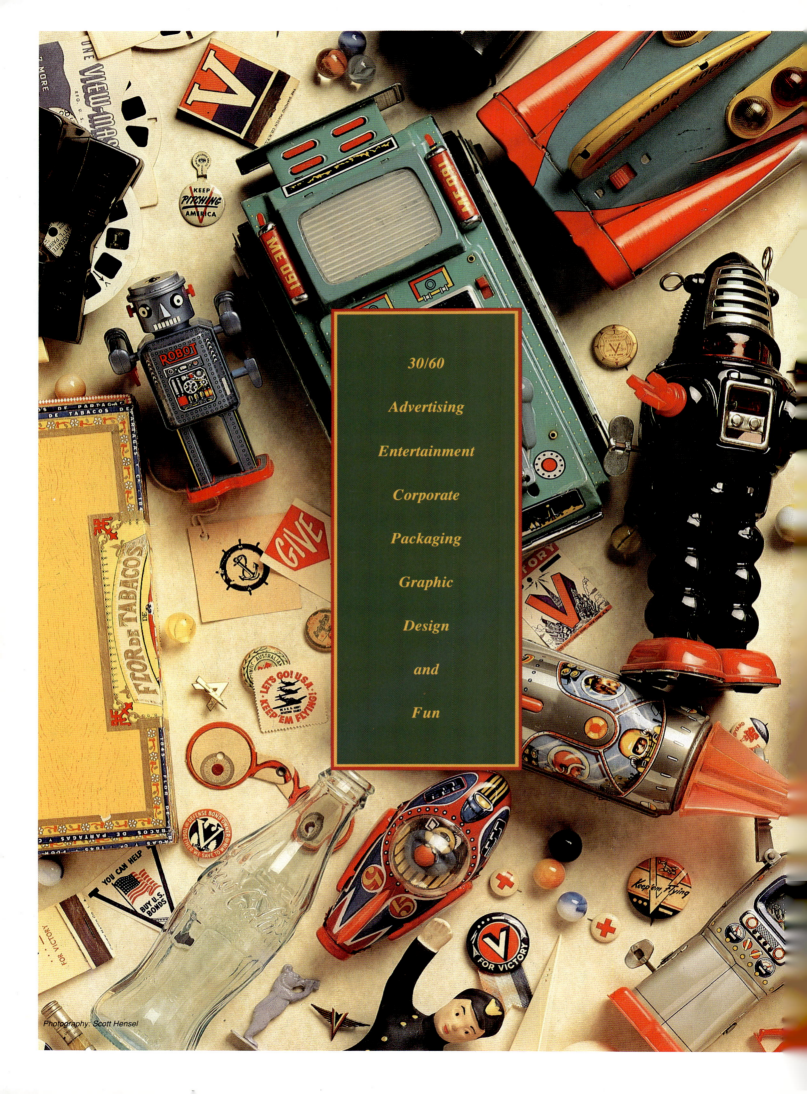

30/60

Advertising

Entertainment

Corporate

Packaging

Graphic

Design

and

Fun

Photography: Scott Hensel

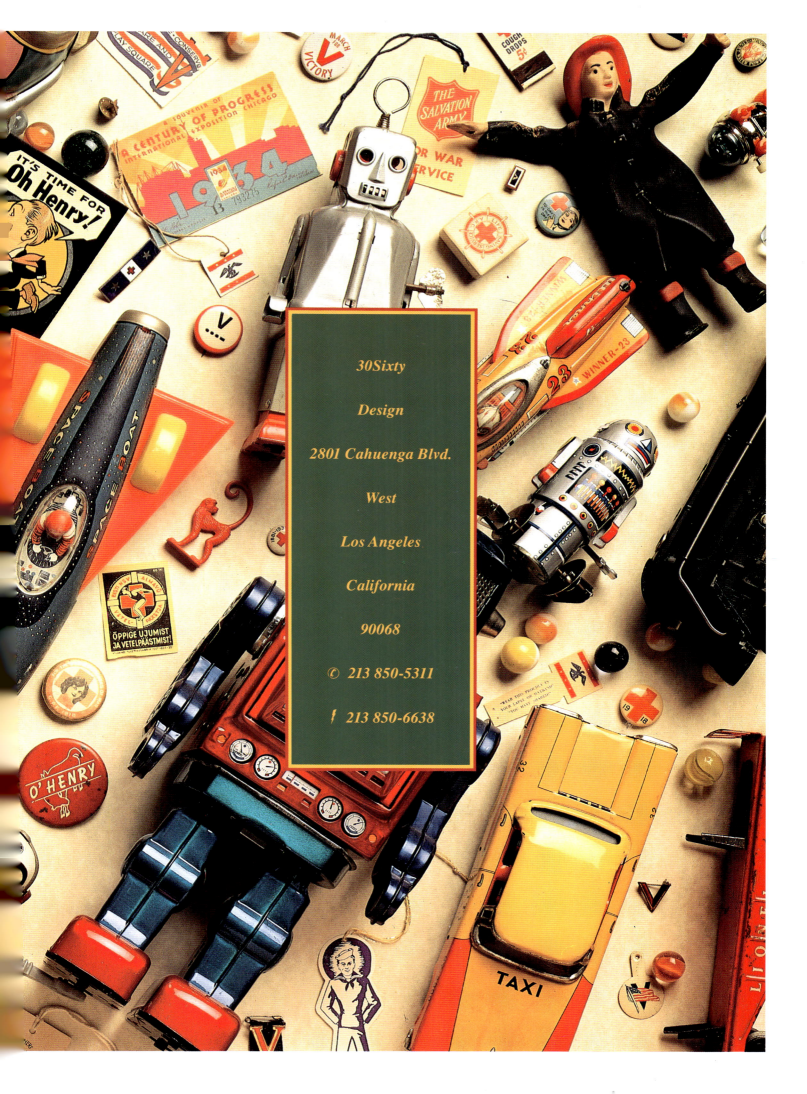

COLOUR GUIDE

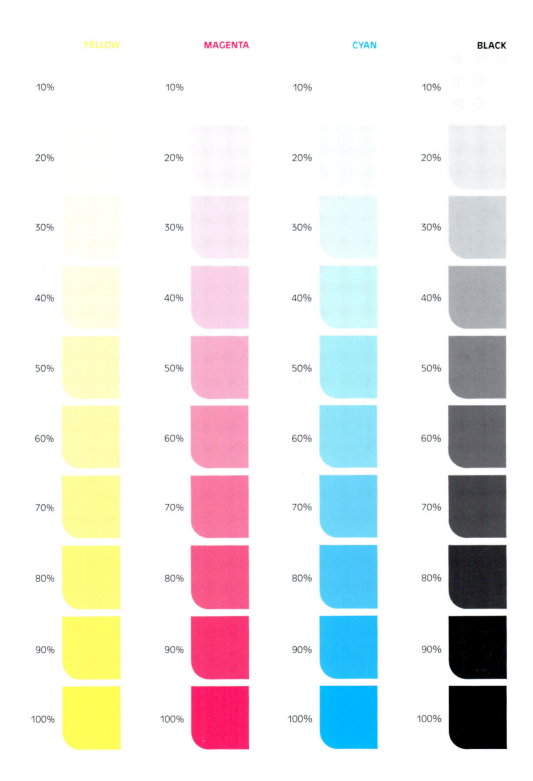

YELLOW	MAGENTA	CYAN	BLACK
10%	10%	10%	10%
20%	20%	20%	20%
30%	30%	30%	30%
40%	40%	40%	40%
50%	50%	50%	50%
60%	60%	60%	60%
70%	70%	70%	70%
80%	80%	80%	80%
90%	90%	90%	90%
100%	100%	100%	100%

Printed by *Everbest* : The choice for colour

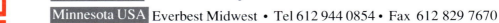

Hong Kong Everbest Printing Co. Ltd • Tel 852 727 4433 Fax 852 772 7687
Ontario Canada Aprinco • Tel 416 286 6688 • Fax 416 286 4931
California USA AsiaPrint Ltd • Tel 714 249 8002 • Fax 714 249 1892
Kentucky USA Four Colour Imports Ltd • Tel 502 456 6033 • Fax 502 473 1437
Minnesota USA Everbest Midwest • Tel 612 944 0854 • Fax 612 829 7670

YELLOW 0

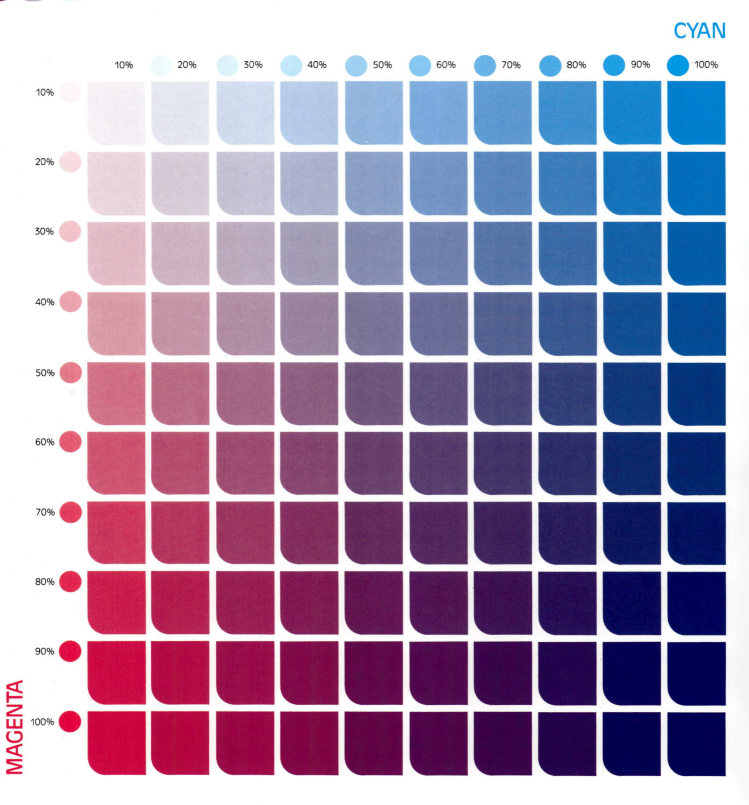

CYAN

MAGENTA

Printed by *Everbest* : **The choice for colour**

Hong Kong Everbest Printing Co. Ltd • Tel 852 727 4433 Fax 852 772 7687
Ontario Canada Aprinco • Tel 416 286 6688 • Fax 416 286 4931
California USA AsiaPrint Ltd • Tel 714 249 8002 • Fax 714 249 1892
Kentucky USA Four Colour Imports Ltd • Tel 502 456 6033 • Fax 502 473 1437
Minnesota USA Everbest Midwest • Tel 612 944 0854 • Fax 612 829 7670

YELLOW 10

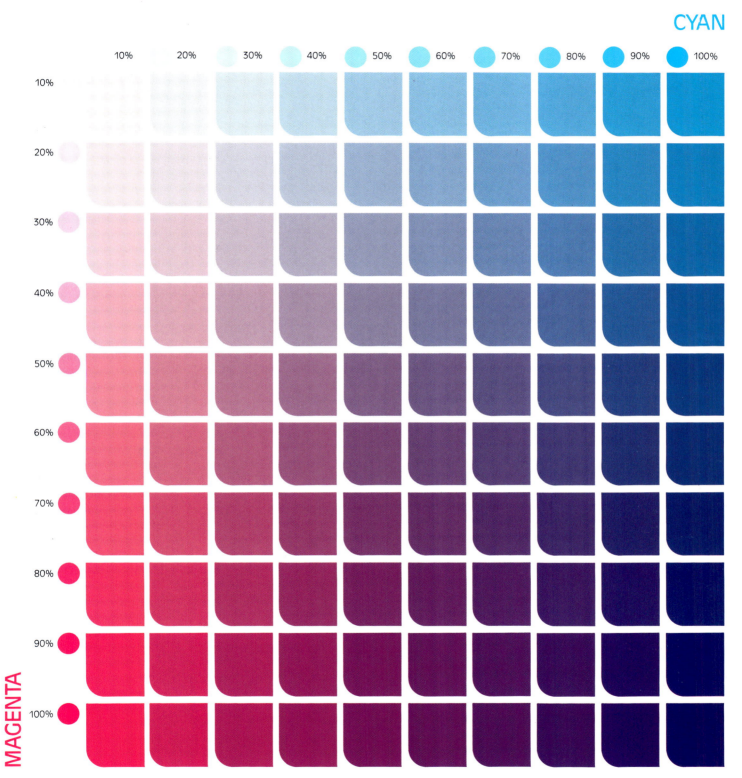

CYAN

10% 20% 30% 40% 50% 60% 70% 80% 90% 100%

MAGENTA

10%
20%
30%
40%
50%
60%
70%
80%
90%
100%

Printed by *Everbest* : 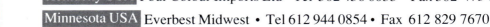 The choice for colour

Hong Kong Everbest Printing Co. Ltd • Tel 852 727 4433 Fax 852 772 7687

Ontario Canada Aprinco • Tel 416 286 6688 • Fax 416 286 4931

California USA AsiaPrint Ltd • Tel 714 249 8002 • Fax 714 249 1892

Kentucky USA Four Colour Imports Ltd • Tel 502 456 6033 • Fax 502 473 1437

Minnesota USA Everbest Midwest • Tel 612 944 0854 • Fax 612 829 7670

YELLOW 20

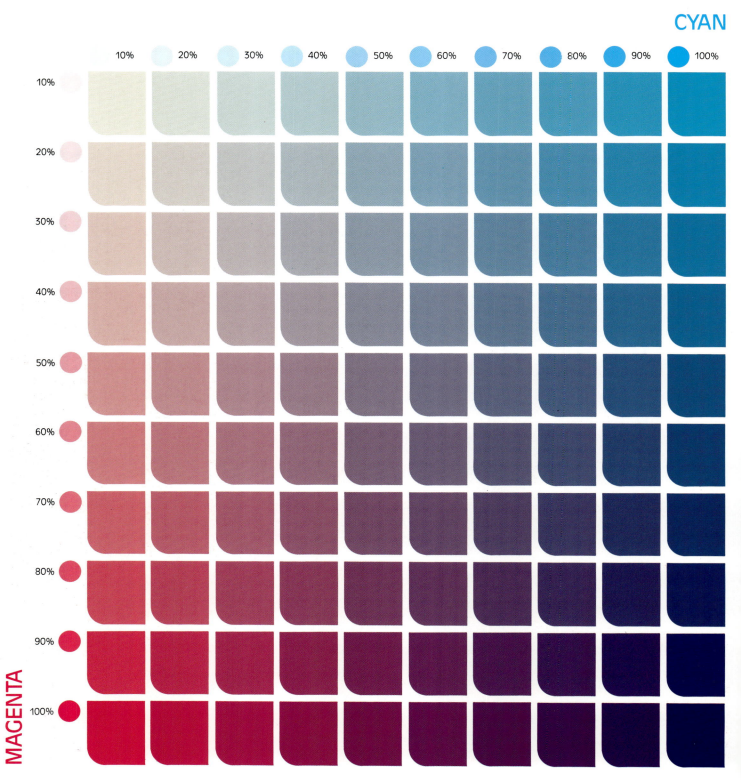

CYAN

MAGENTA

Printed by *Everbest* : **The choice for colour**

Hong Kong Everbest Printing Co. Ltd • Tel 852 727 4433 Fax 852 772 7687
Ontario Canada Aprinco • Tel 416 286 6688 • Fax 416 286 4931
California USA AsiaPrint Ltd • Tel 714 249 8002 • Fax 714 249 1892
Kentucky USA Four Colour Imports Ltd • Tel 502 456 6033 • Fax 502 473 1437
Minnesota USA Everbest Midwest • Tel 612 944 0854 • Fax 612 829 7670

YELLOW 30

CYAN

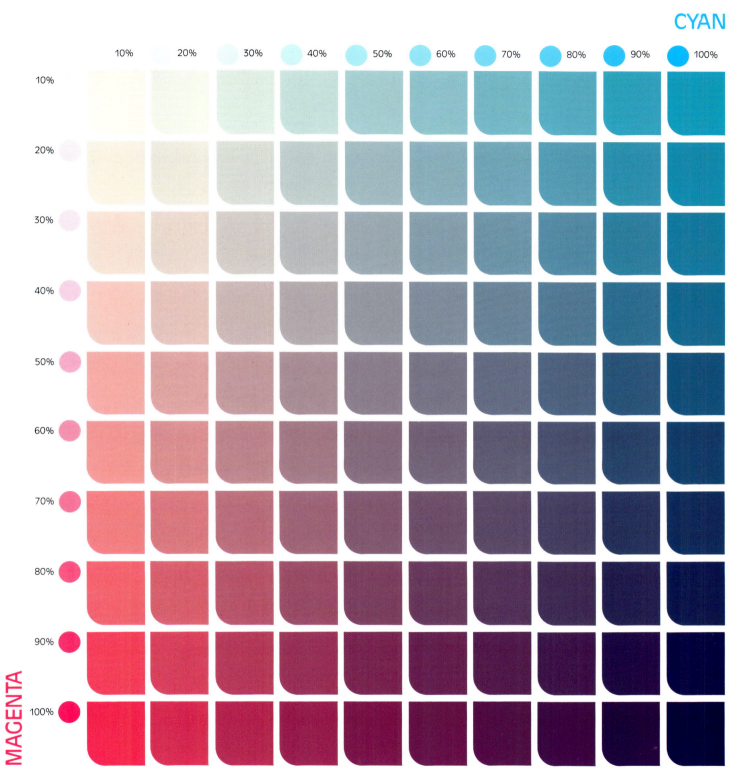

10% 20% 30% 40% 50% 60% 70% 80% 90% 100%

MAGENTA

10% 20% 30% 40% 50% 60% 70% 80% 90% 100%

Printed by *Everbest* : **The choice for colour**

Hong Kong Everbest Printing Co. Ltd • Tel 852 727 4433 Fax 852 772 7687
Ontario Canada Aprinco • Tel 416 286 6688 • Fax 416 286 4931
California USA AsiaPrint Ltd • Tel 714 249 8002 • Fax 714 249 1892
Kentucky USA Four Colour Imports Ltd • Tel 502 456 6033 • Fax 502 473 1437
Minnesota USA Everbest Midwest • Tel 612 944 0854 • Fax 612 829 7670

YELLOW 40

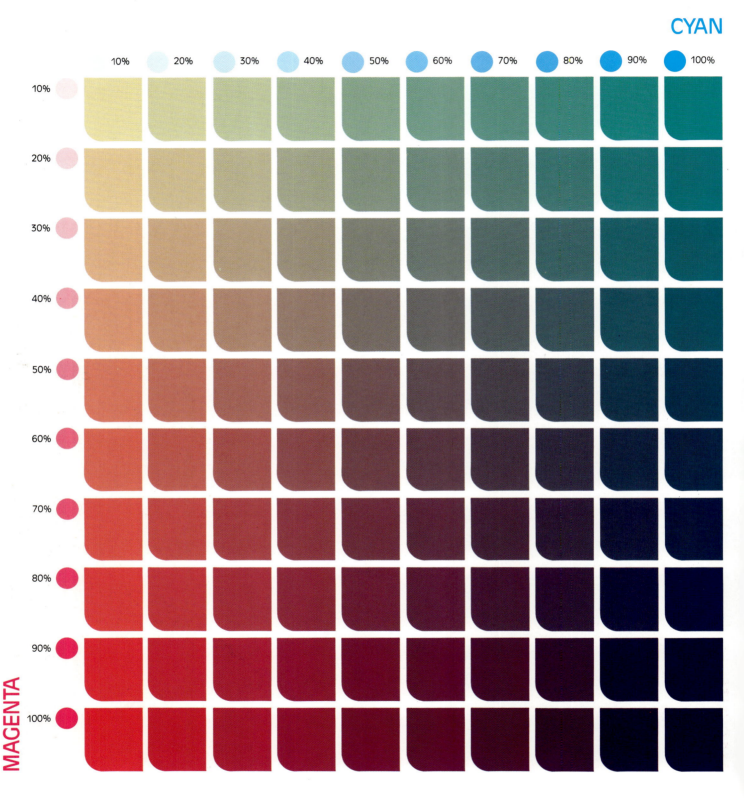

MAGENTA

Printed by *Everbest* : **The choice for colour**

Hong Kong Everbest Printing Co. Ltd • Tel 852 727 4433 Fax 852 772 7687

Ontario Canada Aprinco • Tel 416 286 6688 • Fax 416 286 4931

California USA AsiaPrint Ltd • Tel 714 249 8002 • Fax 714 249 1892

Kentucky USA Four Colour Imports Ltd • Tel 502 456 6033 • Fax 502 473 1437

Minnesota USA Everbest Midwest • Tel 612 944 0854 • Fax 612 829 7670

YELLOW 50

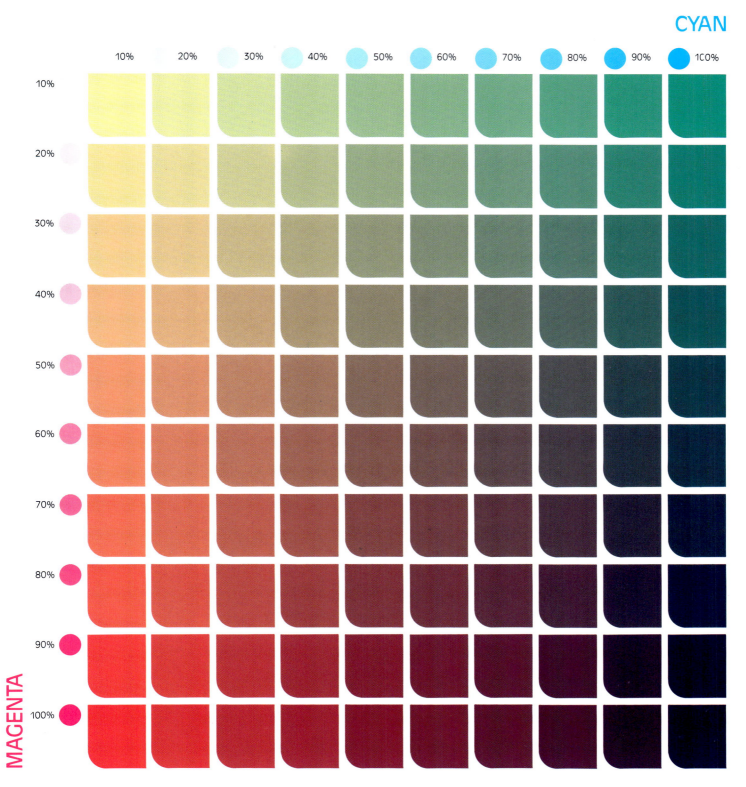

MAGENTA

Printed by *Everbest* : **The choice for colour**

Hong Kong Everbest Printing Co. Ltd • Tel 852 727 4433 Fax 852 772 7687
Ontario Canada Aprinco • Tel 416 286 6688 • Fax 416 286 4931
California USA AsiaPrint Ltd • Tel 714 249 8002 • Fax 714 249 1892
Kentucky USA Four Colour Imports Ltd • Tel 502 456 6033 • Fax 502 473 1437
Minnesota USA Everbest Midwest • Tel 612 944 0854 • Fax 612 829 7670

YELLOW 60

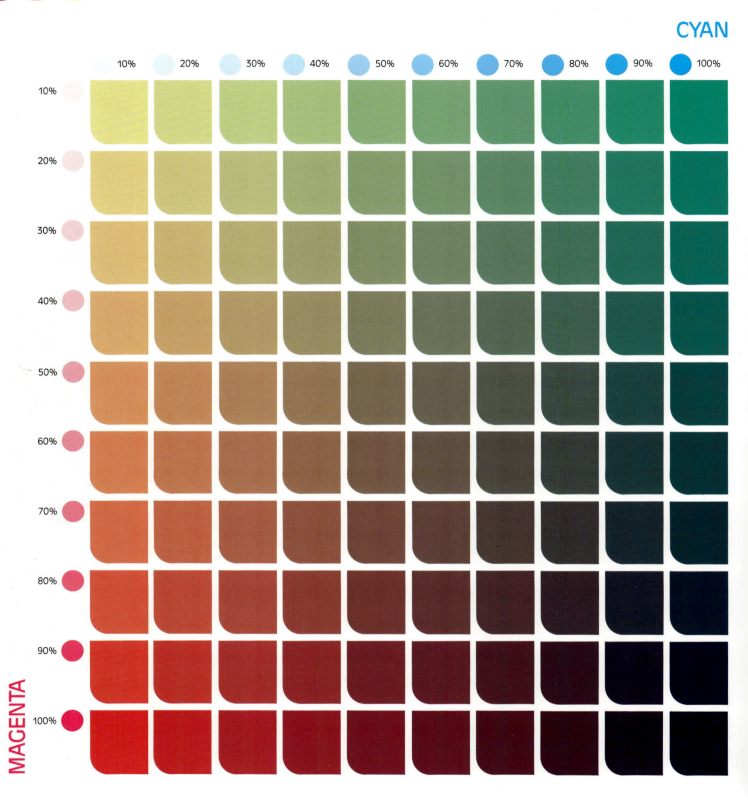

Printed by *Everbest* : The choice for colour

Hong Kong Everbest Printing Co. Ltd • Tel 852 727 4433 Fax 852 772 7687
Ontario Canada Aprinco • Tel 416 286 6688 • Fax 416 286 4931
California USA AsiaPrint Ltd • Tel 714 249 8002 • Fax 714 249 1892
Kentucky USA Four Colour Imports Ltd • Tel 502 456 6033 • Fax 502 473 1437
Minnesota USA Everbest Midwest • Tel 612 944 0854 • Fax 612 829 7670

YELLOW 70

Printed by *Everbest* : The choice for colour

Hong Kong Everbest Printing Co. Ltd • Tel 852 727 4433 Fax 852 772 7687
Ontario Canada Aprinco • Tel 416 286 6688 • Fax 416 286 4931
California USA AsiaPrint Ltd • Tel 714 249 8002 • Fax 714 249 1892
Kentucky USA Four Colour Imports Ltd • Tel 502 456 6033 • Fax 502 473 1437
Minnesota USA Everbest Midwest • Tel 612 944 0854 • Fax 612 829 7670

CYAN

MAGENTA

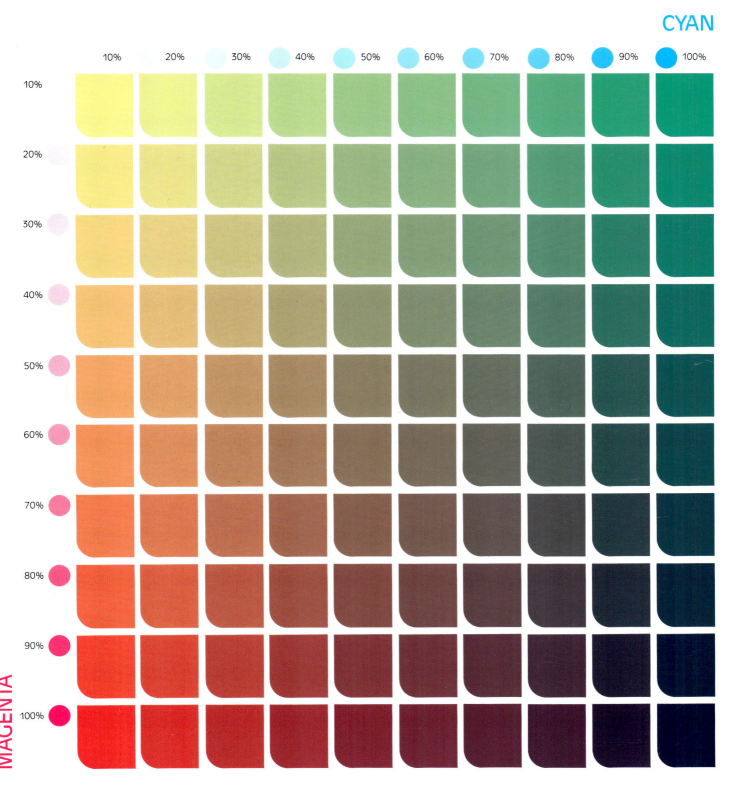

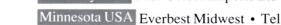

YELLOW 80

CYAN

MAGENTA

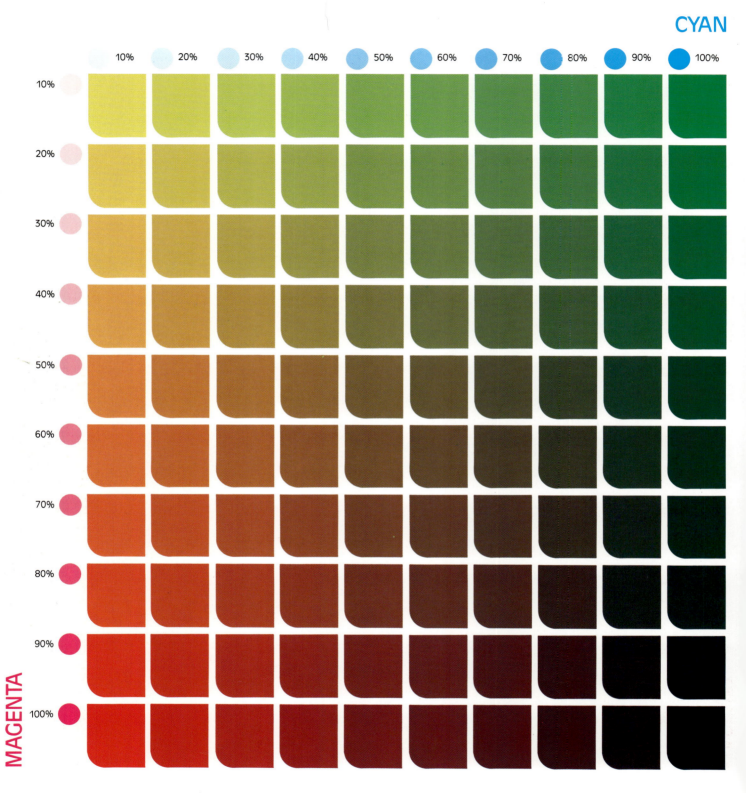

Printed by *Everbest* : The choice for colour

Hong Kong Everbest Printing Co. Ltd • Tel 852 727 4433 Fax 852 772 7687

Ontario Canada Aprinco • Tel 416 286 6688 • Fax 416 286 4931

California USA AsiaPrint Ltd • Tel 714 249 8002 • Fax 714 249 1892

Kentucky USA Four Colour Imports Ltd • Tel 502 456 6033 • Fax 502 473 1437

Minnesota USA Everbest Midwest • Tel 612 944 0854 • Fax 612 829 7670

YELLOW 90

CYAN

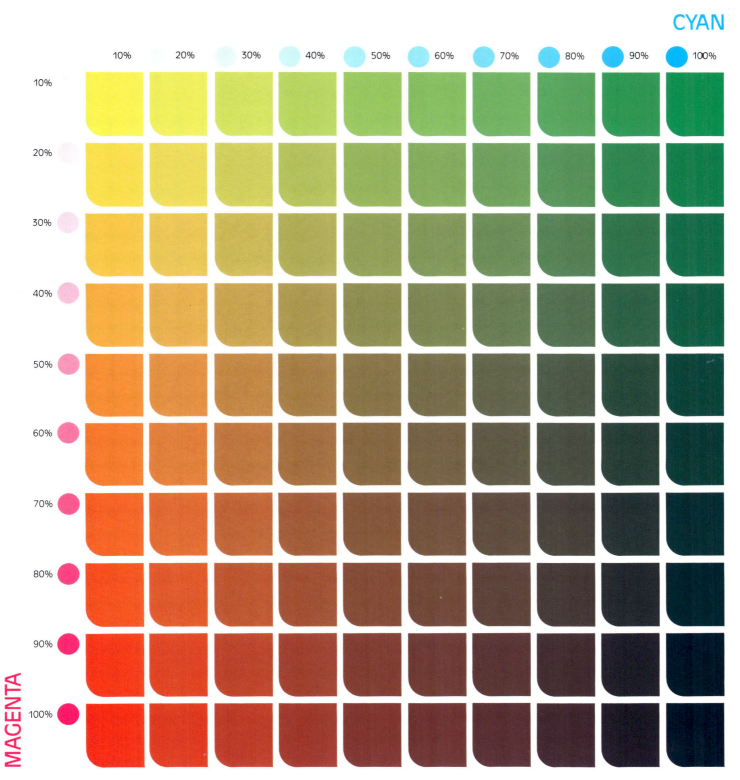

| | 10% | 20% | 30% | 40% | 50% | 60% | 70% | 80% | 90% | 100% |

MAGENTA — 10% 20% 30% 40% 50% 60% 70% 80% 90% 100%

Printed by *Everbest* :   The choice for colour

Hong Kong Everbest Printing Co. Ltd • Tel 852 727 4433 Fax 852 772 7687

Ontario Canada Aprinco • Tel 416 286 6688 • Fax 416 286 4931

California USA AsiaPrint Ltd • Tel 714 249 8002 • Fax 714 249 1892

Kentucky USA Four Colour Imports Ltd • Tel 502 456 6033 • Fax 502 473 1437

Minnesota USA Everbest Midwest • Tel 612 944 0854 • Fax 612 829 7670

YELLOW 100

CYAN

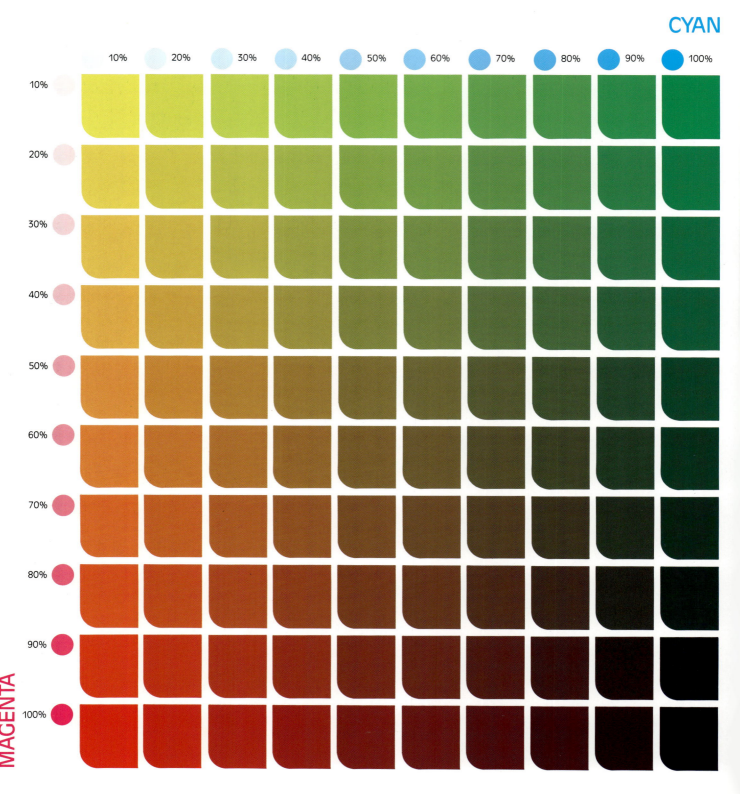

MAGENTA

Printed by *Everbest* : **The choice for colour**

Hong Kong Everbest Printing Co. Ltd • Tel 852 727 4433 Fax 852 772 7687

Ontario Canada Aprinco • Tel 416 286 6688 • Fax 416 286 4931

California USA AsiaPrint Ltd • Tel 714 249 8002 • Fax 714 249 1892

Kentucky USA Four Colour Imports Ltd • Tel 502 456 6033 • Fax 502 473 1437

Minnesota USA Everbest Midwest • Tel 612 944 0854 • Fax 612 829 7670

Y90 + M70

Y100 + M80 + C80

Y30 + M30 + C20 + BL50

Y100 + M20

Y80 + M60 + C40

Y70 + C100 + BL50

Y50 + M70

Y100 + M100 + C70

Y100 + C70

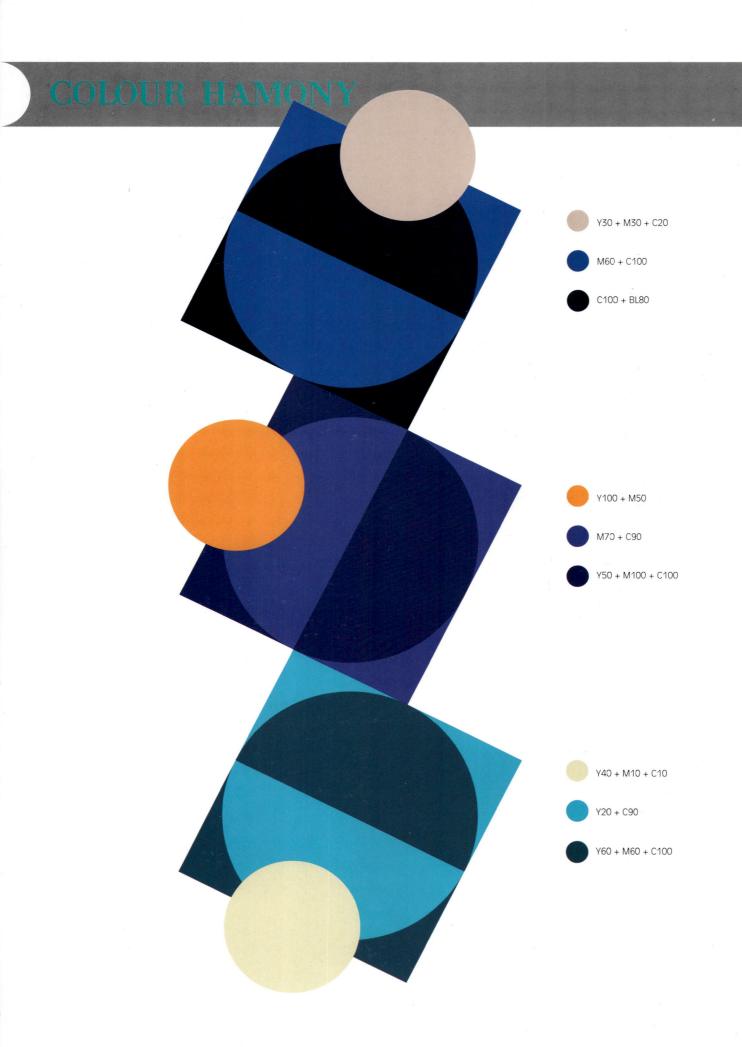

Y30 + M30 + C20

M60 + C100

C100 + BL80

Y100 + M50

M70 + C90

Y50 + M100 + C100

Y40 + M10 + C10

Y20 + C90

Y60 + M60 + C100

Y100 + M100

Y50 + C50 + BL30

Y80 + M100 + C50

Y90 + M80 + C70

Y50 + M70

Y60 + M80 + C90

Y70 + BL30

Y50 + M90 + C30

Y100 + BL90

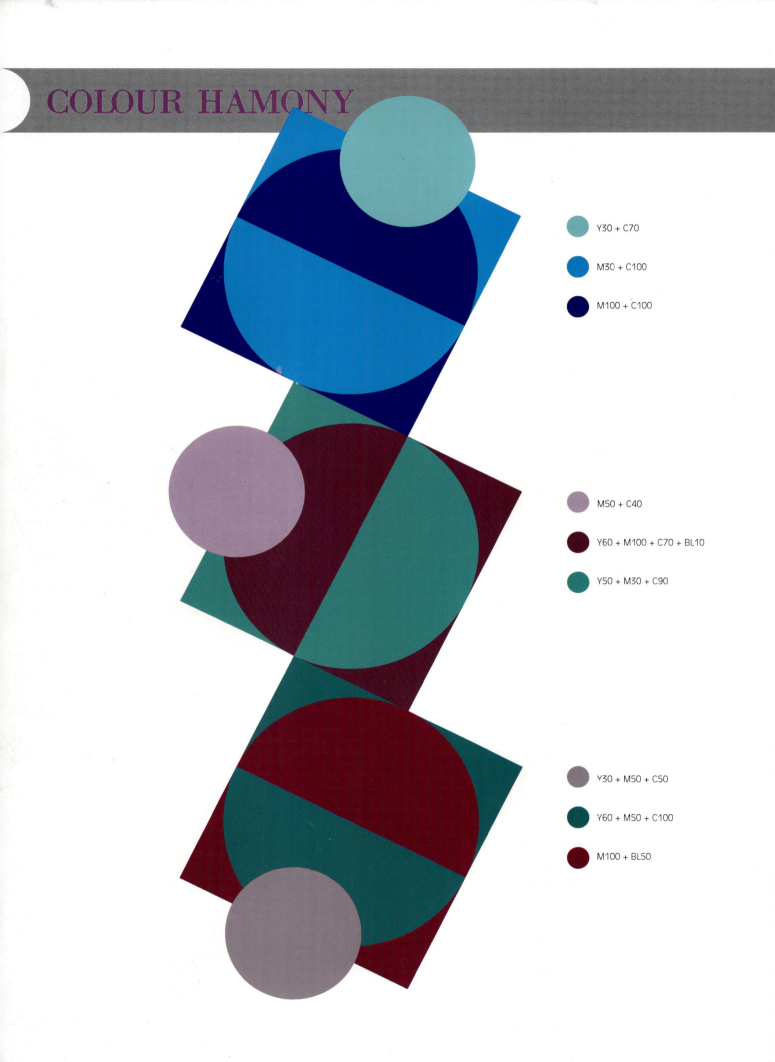

Y30 + C70

M30 + C100

M100 + C100

M50 + C40

Y60 + M100 + C70 + BL10

Y50 + M30 + C90

Y30 + M50 + C50

Y60 + M50 + C100

M100 + BL50